My Child
My Gift

My Child, My Gift has a website!

- ❧ Order copies of *My Child, My Gift*
  (discount available for bulk orders).

- ❧ Submit prayer requests for parents and baby.

- ❧ Share via an interactive on-line forum.

- ❧ Endorse *My Child, My Gift*.

- ❧ Tell your story.

- ❧ Consult our links page.

- ❧ Find new and helpful media resources.

All this and more at www.mychildmygift.com.

Please let us know what online resources have helped you.
What would you like to see?

www.mychildmygift.com

My Child My Gift

A Positive Response to Serious Prenatal Diagnosis

Madeline P. Nugent B.S., M. Ed.
Preface by Mark X. Lowney MD, FACOG
Foreword by Kathy Snow

New City Press
Hyde Park, New York

Published in the United States by New City Press
202 Cardinal Rd., Hyde Park, NY 12538
www.newcitypress.com
©2008 Madeline Pecora Nugent

Cover design by Durva Correia

Library of Congress Cataloging-in-Publication Data:

Nugent, Madeline Pecora.
   My child, my gift : a positive response to serious prenatal diagnosis /
Madeline Pecora Nugent ; foreword by Kathy Snow ; preface by Mark X.
Lowney.
      p. cm.
   Includes bibliographical references.
   ISBN 978-1-56548-291-3 (pbk. : alk. paper)   1. Prenatal diagnosis
--Psychological aspects.   2. Prenatal diagnosis--Religious aspects--
Christianity.   I. Title.

RG628.N84 2008
618.3'2075--dc22   2007052924

Printed in the United States of America

Contents

Dedicated to baby Joseph.
Had he not been conceived with anencephaly,
this book would never have been written.

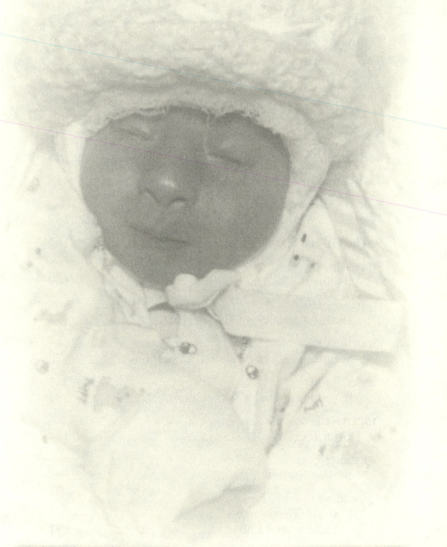

Joseph was diagnosed in utero with anencephaly. He was born at full term and was held and loved by his parents, sister, grandparents, and other relatives for his four days of life after birth.

FORWARD

As a former pro-choice obstetrician-gynecologist who had little regard for the sanctity of human life, it was only through the grace of God that my desire to protect the unborn, and help their mothers at the same time, occurred when I asked the Lord to come into my life in August of 2000. Since then I have dedicated my life to serving God by volunteering as medical director of three pregnancy resource centers: A Woman's Concern, CareNet of Rhode Island, and Woman to Woman Support Network of Middletown, Rhode Island. For years, I have been waiting for a resource which I could offer my patients who face a difficult prenatal diagnosis. My prayers have been answered in Madeline Pecora Nugent's *My Child, My Gift: A Positive Response to Serious Prenatal Diagnosis.*

This book is a comprehensive guide for parents who are unfortunately given the "bad news" regarding their preborn child with either an ultrasound or laboratory diagnosis of a potential or real congenital problem. It explains to them both secular and religious faith-based strategies on how to emotionally, psychologically, and spiritually prepare for and assimilate the multiple and various emotions they will have to reconcile, as well as how to deal with the mixed messages they will be receiving from family members, friends, physicians — and their own inner conflicting feelings.

Madeline utilizes both her personal experience and multitudes of interviews conducted with parents given severe prenatal diagnoses to convey the message given by Jesus Christ, to explain to His disciples why a man was born blind "from birth." They asked Him, "Rabbi, who sinned, this man or his parents, that he was born blind?" Jesus answered, "Neither this man nor his parents sinned; he was born blind so that God's works might be revealed in him" (see Jn 9:1–3).[1]

I have come to believe that every life is precious in the eyes of God and should be also in the eyes of man. God is sovereign over all life and has an eternal purpose for all His creation. King David clearly declared God's love for all preborn children when he wrote:

---

1. Scripture cited throughout the book is from the New Revised Standard Version (Anglicized Edition).

7

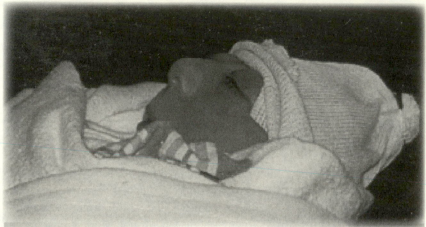

Arianna was diagnosed in utero with anencephaly. Dr. Mark Lowney supported her parents throughout their pregnancy. Arianna was born at full term, was able to feed a bit, responded to her parents' voices, and had many visitors. She lived four days of pure love.

"For it was you who formed my inward parts;
you knit me together in my mother's womb.
I praise you, for I am fearfully and wonderfully made.
Wonderful are your works that I know very well."
(Ps 139:13–14)

I would like to thank Madeline for her relentless love for life, especially the life of the preborn with a severe prenatal diagnosis. Her passion to "[s]peak out for those who cannot speak" (Prv 31:8) is completed by her love and compassion for the parents who are struggling to "defend the rights of the poor and needy" (Prv 31:9).

May God continue to bless richly her and her mission to convince mankind of God's moral will regarding the sanctity of life which is found throughout His Word beginning in Exodus when He declared, "do not kill the innocent or those in the right, for I will not acquit the guilty" (Ex 23:7).

For His Eternal Glory,
Mark X. Lowney MD, FACOG
Fall River, Massachusetts
May 16, 2007

PREFACE

All human life is precious, and the birth of a new baby is just cause for wild and exuberant celebration. Sadly, however, the birth of a baby considered "different," as a result of one or more medical diagnoses, is often perceived as a "tragedy" by medical professionals and many in general society. As a result, the usual new-baby celebration is quashed, along with the hopes and dreams of the baby's parents. When a baby's potential differences are diagnosed *before* birth, the situation devolves even further: physicians, other experts, and even family members often urge the mother and father to terminate the pregnancy. Little thought is given to the joys and contributions this baby may bring to his or her family, or to the world in general. Instead, the focus is on "protecting" parents from the anticipated disappointment, grief, medical bills, or other difficulties this child's birth may cause.

But on a daily basis, the love, concern, and joy of parents whose children are born with disabilities or differences explode the myth that parents need to be "protected." These children — regardless of how long they live and regardless of their medical diagnoses — can bring joy to their families and make the world a better place, by teaching all whose lives they touch. In this book, Madeline shares the stories of many of these parents and their precious children.

This book can enlighten not only parents and extended family members, but also medical personnel and others who hold positions of influence. And I hope this book will cause us to examine the perceptions that drive our actions. Consider, for a moment, the physician who recommends the termination of a baby with disabilities or differences. He believes he is doing "what is best" for the parents and the baby — a baby who is believed to have no potential. But what would this same physician do, for example, if his own two-year-old child were injured in a car accident or were diagnosed with a serious medical condition? Would the doctor not demand that everything possible be attempted in order to save his child's life? Why is the life of a baby not yet born or a newborn any less valuable than his two-year-old child's life? Would the doctor not continue to have hope, regardless of others' opinions? Would he want others to "protect" him from the disappointment, grief, or other difficulties his child's condition might cause?

Deep soul-searching is necessary for us to eliminate the beliefs that the life of an unborn or a newborn baby is less valuable than others. Who has a crystal ball? Who can predict the future? Who can know, with absolute certainty, that a diagnosis is correct, that having a certain condition means the baby will live or die, or that a baby will never achieve this or that? No one has the right to deny a child and his or her family the hopes, dreams, and joys that are inherent to human life. And in my twenty years of experience in the disability field, I have met many parents whose children have defied the odds, made liars out of professionals, and made their families proud!

When my own son, Benjamin, was born seven weeks prematurely, the physician patted me on the shoulder, his eyes filled with pity, and muttered, "Well, I guess you can take him home and do the best you can.... " Rather than feeling sad, I felt anger — he was insulting my baby son — and I was determined not to let others' opinions nor my son's diagnosis of cerebral palsy (and a few other conditions) rule his life! Today, Benjamin is a successful college student who was just inducted into Phi Theta Kappa, the national honor society for community colleges, and he recently won a national film award. Despite needing a power wheelchair, other assistive technology devices, and a variety of supports and modifications, he has always lived an "ordinary" and very fulfilling life. As a child, he was in "regular" activities, like Cub Scouts, T-ball, and drama classes, and was in general education classrooms at school (instead of being segregated in special education classes). His diagnosis cannot define who he is, nor does it determine his potential!

For too long, our children have been described as having "birth defects." What a poor choice of words — and this choice has frequently resulted in the deaths of many children. In today's society, if we find a "defective" product in our homes, we return it to the store for a replacement or dump it in the trash. A history of language indicates that the word "defective" was not applied to human beings until the birth of the Industrial Revolution. Prior to that time, shoes, as one example, were lovingly made by a cobbler's hands, and each shoe was unique. But with the rise of machinery and assembly lines, all shoes were expected to be "perfect," and those that were not were labeled "defective" and were discarded. Somehow, society began applying that standard to human beings. Our children may be born with congenital disabilities or other conditions, but these certainly do not reflect "birth defects," and our children are not defective.

Some children may only be with us a short time, but their lives and their contributions are no less valuable than children who may live to grow old. I will add my testimony to that of others in this wonderful book: my life and the lives of my husband, daughter, and son have all been enriched because of what we have learned and experienced as a result of my son's condition. There is not one thing I would change about my son: he is perfect just the way he is, *as are all children, regardless of the diagnosis or prognosis.*

Our children need us, and we need our children. Our children also need us to have great expectations for them, for whatever time we are privileged to have them with us. And we need to learn from them — our children are our greatest teachers. Their lives and the lessons in this book provide much-needed enlightenment on the value of all human life.

Kathie Snow, Parent, trainer, and author of
Disability Is Natural: Revolutionary Common Sense
for Raising Successful Children with Disabilities
Woodland Park, Colorado
May 16, 2007

Cate (left), Meghan (middle), and their sister Kelsey who was born with CMTC Syndrome.

Acknowledgements

It is impossible to list all of those who deserve thanks for making this book possible. Those many people include:

All the parents who so generously shared their stories for this book.

All the children whose lives are touched upon in these pages.

All those who have read this book and have given helpful comments and input.

My family members, who supported me in this work.

My parents, who gave me a deep respect for life.

Dr. Mark Lowney and Kathie Snow who so graciously wrote the Forward and Preface to this work.

Mark Gordon, my first editor, who believed enough in the book to want it published.

Gary Brandl and Tom Masters, the current editors, who took up where Mark left off.

All of those who prayed for this effort.

The Holy Spirit Whose influence is in these pages, in the stories told. May He bless you all.

INTRODUCTION

The room was quiet, too quiet. There was not even a sound emanating from the ultrasound machine. The radiologist was avoiding my gaze as she intently studied the screen. I redirected my head, shifting my eyes to my husband. I smiled a hopeful smile. Suddenly, the radiologist turned and bluntly addressed us, "I see gross anomalies with this baby. We'll have to call your doctor." In an instant, my dreams of a beautiful, precious baby evaporated and I was plummeted into a swirling nightmare. Inside, I was drowning, gasping for air, choking on the bitter knowledge that something was very wrong with my baby. Although the sun was shining and all around me bustled with life, the storm inside me raged and torrents of tears rushed into my pillow. Yet God did not abandon me, for, by His grace, I was rescued. I realized that this baby was my child, my gift, to love unconditionally for as long as I would have her.

(Doreen, mom of Gianna who was born
with Trisomy 13 and holoprosencephaly)

Dear Parents,

You have received devastating news that your precious unborn baby has a fatal condition or physical or mental differences. If only you could wake up from this nightmare. If only the diagnosis were wrong. If only your baby could be cured. Your mind races through "if onlys." But there is only "what is."

Now you face "what will be."

You can legally choose to end this pregnancy and, with it, your child's life. Or you can choose to continue this pregnancy until its natural end. Much has been written about ending your pregnancy. This book is about continuing it.

Some People I Knew

When I was in high school, the general practitioner's daughter gave birth to a daughter with Down syndrome complicated by physical conditions. The family nicknamed her Little Pumpkin Head and loved her to pieces until she died while still a youngster.

About that same time, another doctor's wife gave birth to Joey, another child with Down syndrome, who grew into a boy so active that his parents had to heighten the fence around their yard so Joey would not climb over it.

After graduating from college, I taught second grade for three years before marrying my dear husband Jim. In my classes, I taught several children who had learning difficulties and a few with physical differences including one child who used a wheelchair.

When Mikey was diagnosed in utero with cloacal exstrophy, doctors gave him zero chance of survival. However, when Mikey was born, doctors were able to correct his condition through several surgeries and, later, a kidney transplant.

In the early 1990s, I saw a photo of a three-year-old child with two lower limb differences and immediately had a sense that we ought to welcome her into our family of four other children. We adopted Kay-Marie who today manages her own floral design business (see www.littleflowerflorals.com).

In 2005, I received a phone call from a friend whose grandson Joseph had been diagnosed in utero with the fatal condition anencephaly. Hospital staff had given her daughter literature about "pregnancy interruption." She asked me to write a booklet about birth. Shortly after agreeing, I met a second couple whose unborn daughter Arianna had been diagnosed with anencephaly. Joseph was born first and lived four days. Arianna was born by cesarean section on her due date. She, too, lived four days. Both children had a stream of hospital visitors, both were fed, both seemed to recognize their mom's voice, both had beautiful funerals followed by potluck dinners, and both forever changed the many people who met them.

Prenatal Diagnosis

Today Down syndrome, physical differences, anencephaly — and over eight hundred other conditions can be diagnosed in utero.[1] As many as 80–90 percent of the parents of these children choose to "interrupt the pregnancies."[2] Those who carry their babies to term are thought to be heroic by some and foolish, deluded, or ultrareligious by others. However, such descriptors are wildly inaccurate. These are ordinary parents who are choosing to give their children every possible chance. They know that they would never "interrupt" a child's life after birth, so why do it before? Such parents understand that love, not intelligence, makes us human. They know that physical and mental differences mean adjustments, but that people can live full lives with those adjustments. They sense that their child deserves nurturing, not "an early goodbye" that brings to death.

I only wish that, before I die, I can get across to one person that they must not close the door on the gift of their child who is different. They are being given something wonderful. The doctors say, "Let's do an amnio. Let's see if the baby is missing brain cells." What are brain cells? So what if Joey had a minimum-sized brain? He could give love, and love is what matters. If I had to do it all over, I would. People say, "What did I do to deserve this child? Did I do something wrong?" My two children, who have handicaps, have helped me grow spiritually. Today folks look upon suffering as bad. The suffering you embrace is the suffering of the diagnosis, of professionals and other people who think you should just end it all now. I look at all these people and I think, "You are not blessed like I have been blessed."

*(Erin, mom of Joey who was born with Trisomy 18
and Patrick who was born with autism)*[3]

---

1. See David D. Weaver and Ira K. Brandt, *The Catalog of Prenatally Diagnosed Conditions, 3ʳᵈ ed.* (Baltimore, Maryland: The John Hopkins University Press, 1999 with periodic updates).

2. Trudy Johnson, "When a Pregnancy Test Shows Down Syndrome" (Focus on the Family Ireland, 2006), http://www.family.ie/marriage/downs.html.

3. Stories shared by parents are in their own words. Some stories have been condensed.

Coming Out of the Closet

While collecting stories for this book, I received an email asking if the book would be "pro-life." One couple did not want to share their story about bringing their baby to birth unless I planned to discuss termination as an equal "loving choice." As the parent of four living biological children, four miscarried children, and one adopted child with limb differences, I know a little about parenting. Here is a condensed form of my reply:

Since 1974, I have counseled women in pregnancy crisis including some who chose termination. Every woman who faces a crisis pregnancy is under extreme pressure, and the desire to "get things back to normal" can be overwhelming. I know the fear, pain, and despair that these women feel and understand how much support they need. I have seen the end results of all choices — continuing the pregnancy and raising the child, adoption, and terminating — and I honestly believe that termination goes against a woman's strongest instinct to nurture and protect her young. Termination is chosen out of terrible fear and lack of external and internal supports, but it violates the female soul.

Having grown up on a farm, I have seen dogs and cows give birth and nurture dead young, trying to get them to nurse and to rise. I have never seen an animal destroy its injured or dying young. When the mother animal finally realizes that the young is dead, she begins to whine, low, or moan in instinctive mourning. We humans are mammals, too. Our female instinct is strong. In nature, no woman would destroy her young, no matter how sick or different they were. She would do all she could to nurture and sustain them.

For women who terminate, I feel only love and compassion. But I cannot say that termination is a good option. I know women may think that it is because doctors, family, society, and even the women themselves can list good-sounding reasons why causing the baby's death is preferable to letting him live. But "head" reasons fail to reach the heart of the woman who aches instinctively to protect and nurture. When a woman terminates, more than her baby dies. Something very primitive and tenderly beautiful dies in the mother. And something very primitive and tenderly beautiful is taken away from the rest of us.

I know that women who terminate often say they are at peace. They say they made a loving choice and have no regrets. They may feel that way until they die. But I have seen too many other women push past the rhetoric and fall apart because they terminated years earlier. Termination ends a life that could have gone on much longer. We do not know what gifts that child would have brought in those subsequent days, and that is the question that eventually lodges in a mother's heart. Conversely, I have been unable to find one mother who continued her pregnancy in the face of adverse prenatal diagnosis who later regretted her decision.

Love and Sacrifice

Life is a great web in which one plucked strand reverberates throughout the whole. Everything in nature, including the human spirit, grows stronger through adversity. When parents trust more than they fear and allow their babies to be born, we all grow a little stronger in our commitment to one another.

Human mothers are not assembly line workers who allow only perfect products to pass inspection. Each baby is unique and precious to the mother. To deny, minimize, or ignore a mother's instinct to nurture and protect her young, no matter how different a child might be, is to war against her soul.

Women are stronger and wiser than society wants to believe. Women humanize the world because they know how to truly love. Love demands sacrifice, and mothers know all about sacrifice. A mechanistic, pragmatic, worldly mind cannot understand why a woman would continue a pregnancy with a baby who has certain difficulties. But love sees more clearly than reason. Reason looks with the mind: but love looks with the heart.

Jennifer followed her heart with Mikey.

When I was twenty weeks pregnant, we learned that our worst fears had come true. Mikey's condition was diagnosed as cloacal exstrophy, an extremely rare birth defect affecting the bladder, urethra, genitalia, large intestine, spine, and lower extremities. In addition, he had a kidney that had stopped growing and functioning. It was recommended that we terminate the pregnancy. We decided to continue on. During my twenty-eighth week of pregnancy, a follow-up ultrasound detected no amniotic fluid. We were informed that Mikey's only functioning kidney had quit working. They told us to expect to lose Mikey in the womb or within days of his birth. They reminded me that termination might be better than continuing on. With consultation from a neonatologist and perinatologist, we made the decision to go to term and to deliver vaginally. Doctors couldn't see any benefit to delivering via C-section. It was also determined that it would be best not to monitor the baby during birth. They didn't want to find the baby in distress and have to do an emergency C-section for a baby who wouldn't live. The anxiety I experienced is indescribable. I prayed that I would make the right decisions. I feared that I'd bring a child into the world who would only live to experience pain and suffering, and I ached to welcome him into a world of love and comfort. I wondered if it would be more peaceful for the baby to end things, but the thought of not giving him a chance was devastating. I tried to put my religious beliefs aside to make unbiased choices. However, I learned quickly that I had to entrust my son's fate to God. I just wasn't big enough for this. The doctors assured me that they would keep our son pain-free and that he'd always be peaceful. It brought me great comfort to know that I still held hope for my unborn son and that I had entrusted his life to God.

All I remember is utter silence when Mikey was born. I thought he had died. The doctors whisked Mikey to the corner of the room, assessing the situation. A few minutes later, we heard a faint cry. I'll never forget the relief I felt. A nurse brought Mikey over to us. I can hardly remember anything but trying so hard to engrain the memory of his face in my mind. He was a beautiful baby, and I thought that this may be the only time I would ever see him. A team of surgeons operated and found that his bowel had attached to his bladder. He was born without an anus, so they made a colostomy. He also had a mild form of spina bifida, so the neurosurgeons untethered his spinal cord. The doctors still say they've never seen an anatomy quite like Mikey's. My amniotic fluid was gone because Mikey was recycling it through his own little body. His only good kidney was indeed working. I will never forget the day the nephrologist told us, "This kid is going to make it!" My husband and I were completely dumfounded. It was our happiest moment ever!

I am glad that we gave our child the chance he deserved. Today, Mikey is an amazing boy, doing all the normal things that kids do. If we didn't tell someone about his "problem" they would never know that he wasn't "normal." Mikey has brought a joy to our lives that we never knew before. Even if Mikey had not made it, I could live with myself as I did everything possible to leave matters in God's hands. It was a maternal decision. I am responsible as his mother for giving him every opportunity possible. I am responsible for protecting this child while I am pregnant with him. What is the value of each life? God makes those decisions. He decides how long you are going to live. There is a reason for that baby being there. Mikey opened so many closed doors. He made me a more compassionate person. I don't look at situations the way I used to. You really understand the value of life and the value of each day after you go through something like this. I was listening to a country western song about a guy who gets diagnosed with something or other. He said, "Wouldn't it be great if everyone lived life like it was their last day?" That makes sense to me. We don't know how many days we have with Mikey so we try to make each day an incredible day.

(Jennifer, Mikey's mom)

At age four-and-a-half Mikey's kidney failed and he underwent dialysis and then a kidney transplant with one of his father's kidneys. Mikey did well following the surgery. However, not every story in this book ends with a living child. This book is not about babies who live and babies who die. It is about giving babies a chance to live as long as they can. Jennifer and her husband gave Mikey that chance.

Unexpected Gift

A serious prenatal diagnosis robs you of the image of the baby you dreamed of — the "perfect child." But you never had that baby. You always had the baby you have now. An older book on parenting a child with a disability states, "You can believe that your child's condition is a death blow to everything you've dreamed and worked toward until now. Or you can decide that you will continue to lead the life you'd planned — and incorporate your child into it."[4] Or you can trust that the future will be better than what you planned because this particular child will be in it.

> Luke's life was a journey without end. There has been much more joy than sorrow, believe it or not. I miss my baby, but he did have a wonderful life. All he knew was love, and he accomplished his purpose of being sent to this earth. We try to continue to share his message of God's love for us and our need to accept His plan for our life and not fight against this plan. For those of you starting this journey, you will never be the same. You will be better. It is a hard journey, but our babies are more than worth the effort. We don't look back in regret. We continue to look up in faith. God Bless.
>
> *(Sue, mom of Lucas Adam who was
> born with anencephaly)*[5]

> If you had told me years ago that we would go through this, I would have thought I would have gone crazy, I couldn't do it. But once we were in it, then strength that was not of us was given to us. It wasn't about having a positive attitude. It was about purifying my heart so God could be present and to allow myself to believe in His power.
>
> *(Mimi, mom of Claire who was misdiagnosed in utero
> as having fatal encephalocele)*

---

4. Robin Simons, *After the Tears: Parents talk about raising a child with a disability* (Denver, Colorado: Children's Museum of Denver, 1985), preface (np).

5. Mimi Citeralla, "Fighting for Claire: Battling Not a Disease but a Culture," in *Called to Greatness* (Spring 2007): 6. This is the newsletter of Sisters of Life, Yonkers, New York. See http://www.sistersoflife.org/.

Today's strength is enough for today. Strength for tomorrow will be given when tomorrow comes. Look through the lens of a mother's love to bring your child as far as he or she can go. Do not be afraid. Trust your instincts and fight for your child. This book, and the parents who share herein, will support you.

Madeline Pecora Nugent

1
FINDING OUT

Endure and persist. This pain will turn to your good by and by.[1]

Ovid

Jonathan

> I have a plan for Jonathan
> Beyond all wishes and dreams.
> I have a plan for Jonathan
> Greater than all that seems.
>
> When I created the universe
> Jonathan was joy in my mind.
> Singing our song of creation,
> United to all mankind.
>
> ....
> Together we embrace all love
> And pain of every kind;
> Our plan of love for everyone,
> Transforming all mankind.
>
> To know the gift of Jonathan
> Is to know his life in me.
> Fantastic love! Fantastic joy!
> For all eternity.
>
> ....

> *Monsignor James A. Brassil, selections from a poem for*
> *Jonathan Dobkowski who was born with Potter's Syndrome*[2]

You or someone you know has received a serious prenatal diagnosis. How can you cope with the unsettling transition from where you were before the diagnosis to where you must go? Perhaps the way to begin is to know that others have been where you are.

Unexpected News

Learning that your unborn child has significant differences catapults you into a parallel universe where you are dealing with crisis and uncertainty, while everyone else seems blissfully happy.

---

1. http://thinkexist.com/quotation/endure_and_persist-this_pain_will_turn_good_by/148949.html.

2. http://www.angelfire.com/ny5/jonathandobkowski/Poems.html. Used with permission.

Celine is our second child. When I became pregnant with her, my first child was only five months old. This caused me a bit of stress, since I was still adjusting to a new baby, and the idea of another one was overwhelming. Maybe because I was preoccupied with my own feelings, I was not really enthusiastic about the OB visits, the ultrasounds, shopping for baby things, etc. All of this changed at our twenty-two-week ultrasound. Suddenly, the baby became the center of my universe.

(Monica, mom of Celine who was born
with hypoplastic right heart syndrome)

When you went for your first routine ultrasound, you were probably expecting to learn the baby's gender[3] and size. You never thought something might be "wrong" with your baby.

We were so relieved to see our baby moving. The tech pointed out the heart and spine and everything except for the brain. She went to look for the doctor. We stayed in the room talking about all our plans for this child. The doctor walked in and said, "Your baby has anencephaly. The brain never formed." My world stopped. I remember asking if this meant our baby could die and she said yes, it would definitely die. I can't even begin to write of the emotions of that day or of the pain.

(Sue, mom of Lucas Adam who
was born with anencephaly)

I was rather anxious before the ultrasound — I just wanted to make sure everything was OK. You know, count the fingers and toes and watch him (or her) wiggle and kick. I figured it was normal anxiety and I was being silly. Little did I know. The technician kept looking for kidneys in the baby and couldn't find them. That's when my heart started breaking. The doctor threw out a few words like Potter's and oligohydramnios. Potter's is a condition that is completely incompatible with life outside the womb. She told us, "You will survive, though it will be a tough road." We saw tears in her eyes, too. We were scheduled for a more detailed ultrasound. I don't remember anything except crying in my husband's arms. We were in shock. We closed in to ourselves and told everyone that the ultrasound had been rescheduled. We had to absorb the situation some first.

(Anna, mom of Joshua who
was born with Potter's Syndrome)

When you receive a serious prenatal diagnosis, you are overcome with anger, confusion, disbelief, denial, or grief.

We were told that our baby had an "incompatible with life" condition, hypoplastic left heart syndrome (HLHS). The OB offered us a

---

3.   This book will use male or female pronouns randomly.

few options, including termination. I could not believe my ears. I recall an immediate surge of defiance flowing up in me. It was incomprehensible to me that the OB could so dispassionately tell us we could terminate, as though we could just give up on our baby and move on with our lives. I searched her face, her eyes, looking for some small glimmer of appreciation of the weight of the news she had just delivered. It was in vain. It was time to move on, alright. I never saw her again.

(Monica, mom of Celine who was born
with hypoplastic right heart syndrome)

You may wish you were dead or that your baby were. You may try to bargain with God. "Let it be me instead of my baby." Your mind is too numb to process the information. How can you survive the next twenty-four hours much less the distant future? How can you endure the waiting?

I spent hours on the internet looking at Trisomy 18, and everything pointed to the fact that our baby was most likely to be stillborn, or if she were born alive, she would likely live only days, hours, or even minutes. How do I even deal with this? I spent a lot of time hugging my other children, praying, and of course, crying. The praying was hard, because I didn't know what to pray for. The emotions were really intense, and they kept changing. I was amazed at how angry I was about being pregnant and how much I hated it at that moment. I felt like it was a constant reminder that my baby was going to die. It seemed like such a waste to be pregnant when my baby was going to die. And it was almost unbearable to think about those who didn't know and who were going to ask me cheerful questions about the pregnancy. How could I endure this? I just wanted it to be over. Eventually, I got exhausted from crying and actually felt a lot better. Later that evening, searching the internet as usual, I found the "Carrying to Term" pages and saw a section about early emotions that said that it is common to hate the pregnancy for awhile, but that it would pass quickly. That made me feel better (hopeful) about it, and that feeling did pass in a couple of days.

(Mindy, mom of Abigail who was
born with Trisomy 18)

That night I was haunted by horrific visions. I tried to pray and find comfort, but I would wake up and want to flee. I kept thinking of my baby's nose; we were told that, besides the holoprosencephaly, our daughter had no nose. How would I ever find the courage to gaze upon my daughter at her birth? I had no strength to persevere and my tears flowed incessantly. I wanted to run and run and bring along a preterm labor so I could be done. I felt so alone.

(Doreen, mom of Gianna who was born
with Trisomy 13 and holoprosencephaly)

You need time to process the diagnosis without making any decisions until you can think clearly.

> The doctor described what our daughter would look like at birth (a description which proved to be accurate). I was in shock. At that moment, if they had taken me to an abortion room, I would have trusted them that they were doing what was best. As it was, the doctor said, "Go home and think about how the baby is different."
>
> *(Patricia, mom of Jessica who was born*
> *with limb differences of both arms and both legs)*

You may be in what one parent called "nothingness." Nothing exists in your mind except your child.

> When I received my baby's diagnosis, the book they gave me was full of a lot of stories of people who terminated their pregnancies and only a couple of stories of people who carried their babies to term. It was hard not knowing/realizing that other mothers out there Do carry their babies, too. It seems so hard to plan on carrying to term anyhow right after the diagnosis, but with time it becomes doable. Moms need to give themselves some time before making their own decision. For me, the experience of carrying Joyann to term was worth it all. I enjoyed my time with her so much. I never regret a moment.
>
> *(Jewell, mom of Joyann who*
> *was born with anencephaly)*

Your feelings toward other pregnant women and healthy babies may have suddenly changed.

> Right after the diagnosis, I was sitting in the waiting area. Another woman walked in, obviously pregnant. Normally I would have asked her how far along she was. I did not. I just had this sudden awareness that I was now in a different club than she was. She was still bright with expectations; all my hopes of caring for a child had just been taken away. To have started a conversation would have just distressed her. Oddly, I did not really envy her, nor did I resent other women who carried newborns in the grocery store. I did not begrudge them their children, but I did look at them and wish that my daughter might have the chance to do childish things with me. Seeing them sometimes caused me to feel saddened or wishful, and to wonder if they really knew how much of a miracle a child is.
>
> *(Laura, mom of Sidney who was born*
> *with a lethal form of dwarfism)*

I had a hard time with obviously pregnant women. I hated my doctor's appointments. I would go in praying to still hear a heartbeat but also wanting this nightmare to be over.

(Sue, mom of Lucas Adam
who was born with anencephaly)

Imagine the worst-case scenario and picture yourself dealing with that. Then you will feel prepared.

Self-Blame

You may ask, "Am I responsible for this?"

The radiologist said, "Here is his nose, here are his eyes, and normally you would expect to see a head behind them." What a lousy way to announce the devastating news of anencephaly! I was stunned! I put my hand over my ears and cried out to tell him to stop! I immediately turned to my midwife and said, "Carol, this is all my fault. This is because of the medication I took early in my pregnancy!!!!!"

(Ann Marie, mom of Loren Joseph who
was born with anencephaly)

This was my third baby, and I thought, "What if this is real? How do I tell my family? Will everyone accept her? When she comes out, how will I react?" I kind of fell apart at that point. For a good portion of the evening, I felt as if there was something I did that may have caused it.

(Annalee, mom of Brooke who was born
with nodules for fingers and a boneless thumb on her left hand)

Self-blame is not only unhealthy; it is also false. In Loren's case, many moms took the same medication that Ann Marie had taken and without any serious effect. Brooke was affected by amniotic band syndrome for which there is no known cause and effect.

Mothers who receive excellent prenatal care can have children with significant differences:

Since I had experienced three previous miscarriages and preterm labor in the latter of all my pregnancies, I made sure to take the proper vitamins and eat a healthy diet. At the beginning of my second trimester, I limited my activities to avoid complications of preterm labor. By adhering to this discipline, I believed I would have a healthy child.

(Doreen, mom of Gianna who was born
with Trisomy 13 and holoprosencephaly)

I felt a great need from the beginning of the pregnancy to not do anything that might hurt the baby. I took no meds but Tylenol, ate very healthy, and even went through two miserable sleep studies to get CPAP prescribed to improve my oxygen levels at night. I have the assurance that I did not do anything to add to Sidney's burdens.

(Laura, mom of Sidney who
was born with a lethal form of dwarfism)

Then I heard someone saying, "Anencephaly. Are you familiar with it?" I said immediately, "Yes, but I was taking folic acid.[4] What does this mean?" They said, "Of the babies that are born with anencephaly, only about half of them are born alive. Most are stillborn."

(Jewell, mom of Joyann who
was born with anencephaly)

Time is too precious to waste on self-blame. Blame pulls the focus away from the time you have with your baby.

Questions

You may ask:

- ❧ Are the doctors right?
- ❧ What can be done?
- ❧ What is this going to do to my life? My family? My plans?
- ❧ How am I going to handle this?
- ❧ Is God punishing me?
- ❧ How should I act now?

Then I started having strange thoughts and feelings like maybe my baby wasn't really alive and maybe people would think I wasn't pregnant anymore. I wondered if people would think I shouldn't act pregnant anymore.

(Mary Sue, mom of Luke Daniel who
was born with anencephaly)

You may wonder if you will be able to look at your child.

Yet, practical thoughts worry me: how will we react at the sight of the wounded head? Anouk is born at 5:21 p.m. The midwife just put a little cap on her head and I can finally hold her. She is alive! Is she going to start breathing? The world around me stops and the most important thing is my daughter. Although I clearly know that she is going to die, I am so happy. Joy fills the room around us; joy and

---

4. Doctors prescribe folic acid during pregnancy to help prevent neural tube defects such as anencephaly. See http://www.kidshealth.org/parent/pregnancy_newborn/pregnancy/folic_acid.html.

peace. Anouk starts breathing gently, uncertainly at the beginning, but then in a more and more regular way. She is so tiny, especially her head. She looks like the three others did at the birth. After our parents' visit, I remain alone with Anouk. Now I am ready to have a glance under the bloodstained cap. The wound is awful but belongs to Anouk and does not shock me. The room is so quiet and I am so happy that Anouk is alive, but I must confess that I will be soothed when she dies. She certainly cannot live.

(Monika, mom of Anouk who
was born with anencephaly)

When we were told Sidney had a form of potentially lethal dwarfism, I researched the various conditions that could cause it. Some had very obvious defects: clubfoot, cleft lip, bulgy eyes and forehead, a bloated and swollen body, misshapen limbs, and other very visible and distressing problems. Could I look past the abnormalities and still love my child? This must be one of those unspoken insecurities in many, if not all, parents — can they look at a child, one who looks like people they have pitied or felt revulsion or disinterest toward, and love the baby because he or she is their child? I went online and looked for pictures of babies with the problems mine might have. Some of the defects were horrifying at first. But if I kept looking, then after a moment or two, there was just a baby, and I found my heart was touched. I knew that I COULD love my child. After all, I love the child whom I feel inside me; it is only her exterior I do not yet know.

(Laura, mom of Sidney who
was born with a lethal form of dwarfism)

Hope

You may feel convinced that your baby is going to be fine.

One night Phil came home from work and declared, "Honey, we are going to set up the bassinet and get ready for Maria to come home. If we believe that she will be healed, then God will heal her." I had already made funeral arrangements, but we decided to concentrate on praying for a miracle. I believed that Maria was going to be perfectly normal at birth. "So I tell you, whatever you ask for in prayer, believe that you have received it, and it will be yours," said the Lord (Mk 11:24). I confidently clung to these words. I typed up a novena[5] to Blessed Margaret of Castello, a woman who was cast out by her parents for her severe deformities, and sent it to everyone I know. I asked that they pray it for nine days and if they would like

---

5. A novena is nine days of prayer for a particular request.

to begin it again, all the better. I also requested that they please make copies to pass along to others. We began receiving cards and letters from people we did not know, saying that they were praying for us and for little Maria. This child had hundreds upon hundreds of people on their knees. Maria died in utero about 4:00 p.m. and was born four hours later on December 21, 1995. Maria had spina bifida and a hole the size of my palm in her back. She was also bent at her hands and feet. She resembled the crucified Christ — the One Who came and gave His life for us. I was holding in my arms one who gave of her life for others. How privileged I was to be her mother! Maria lived a perfect life. She existed nine months in her mother's womb and went directly to her Mother and Father in Heaven. She never felt pain or sorrow. She never shed a tear, never had to experience a grueling death. She only knew love, warmth, comfort and peace.

(Terri, Maria D.'s mom)

Maria's parents hoped that Maria would be "perfectly normal." But she was not nor is any child "perfect." Does God not answer prayer? Or does he sometimes give a different answer than the one prayed for?

Journeying with a child with multiple disabilities is a life-prayer. We delight in the silent milestones and learn to take little steps and to delight in them. It is not the apparent, transitory successes that mark the validity of our prayer, but how faithful we are to the journey. And the journey is worth taking — worth embracing — worth living for a lifetime. My son Christopher had contracted beta strep in my womb. Deflated lungs, infection, sepsis, and five weeks in a neonatal facility on 100 percent oxygen would eventually leave him "mentally retarded and crippled for life." I had toxemia and was hospitalized eleven days prior to his birth and I had been on some pretty potent antidepressants during pregnancy. And now God was asking me to trust him and to take care of this child. I had been blessed by a very supportive husband, but he worked sixteen hours a day. And there was so much uncertainty. But God was merciful and loving. He showed us day by day the path we should take. We had to be willing to surrender Christopher's fate to the loving Creator. This child taught us dear lessons about suffering and resilience that have taken us through difficult family times and renewed our love for one another. He would never offend God — he was a living saint. He rarely complained of his disabilities, trusting in God to give him a new back, brain, and legs when "we came back to life again" on the Last Day. I have tried to grow in patience with well-intentioned others who saw me carrying a cross that I knew was sheer blessing. Christopher was that blessing beyond blessings and I could never live without that beatitude in my life or that source of virtue. Amen!

(Mary, Christopher's mom)

Where Is God?

Not every parent believes in God. If you do, you may be angry with God. Tell God your feelings or write him a letter. Seek guidance in your faith.

> One morning I read the following verse: "For the perishable must clothe itself with the imperishable, and the mortal with immortality. When the perishable has been clothed with the imperishable, and the mortal with immortality, then the saying that is written will come true: 'Death has been swallowed up in victory.' 'Where, O death is your victory? Where, O death is your sting?'" (I Cor 15:53–55). Because I believe these words, I will be able to face the following months confidently. It is not the expectation of a miracle which helps me to endure everything, but the assurance of the baby's resurrection and eternal life. What are eighty years of life (if she would live as long as an average person) compared to eternity?
>
> *(Monika, mom of Anouk who*
> *was born with anencephaly)*

Why did this happen? No one can answer that question. But you are asking it because your child's condition seems unfair, even wrong. Yet the strange and wonderful thing about "bad" is that it often brings about "good" that would never have otherwise happened.

> Megan and Kate are much, much better people because of their sister Kelsey. They are nice to kids in school, reaching out to people. Kelsey has really enriched their lives and my entire family and Jack's entire family — they recognize that their lives have totally changed because of Kelsey. She has touched so many people's lives. There was a guy at church we didn't know who came up to us a few years ago with this huge Easter basket and he said, "I just want to tell you, Kelsey, that I come to church every Sunday and I see you with your family. I see you looking up at the lights and talking to your family. You helped me get through this terribly difficult year. I wanted to get you this Easter basket." I was amazed that here was somebody sitting across the church from us that I didn't even know. Kelsey was an inspiration to him. There was a woman in church who introduced her daughter who had disabilities. Her daughter was in her fifties and her mother was in her seventies. The mother came up to us after church and said, "I wanted you to meet my daughter. I've never brought my daughter to church before, but I've been watching you for a long time and I saw that people were accepting your daughter and that gave me the strength to bring my daughter to church." Now I see her regularly there. There was another mother with a daughter who had Down syndrome, who is probably in her thirties. The mother brought her daughter to church regularly. She

saw Kelsey going up with the Confirmation[6] students, and she said
to me after Mass, "Kelsey can make her Confirmation?" I said, "Of
course." She said, "My daughter never did." I said, "Is that something
you think she would like to do?" And she said, "Oh, definitely." So we
got her hooked up so she made her Confirmation along with Kelsey.
All those years ago, it wasn't something people were doing. But now
they see Kelsey and they say, "Why not?"

*(Chylene, mom of Kelsey who
was born with CMTC Syndrome)*

Disability: Natural Part of Life

Being pregnant with a child with a serious condition forces you to look
at how you think.

The beginning of successful lives for children is our unconditional
belief in them and their potential for success. For many parents, this
belief is often conditional, based on conventional wisdom and the
system. For example, a parent may think a child can only be successful if or when he learns to walk, talk, take care of himself, or
whatever. Or we may think success will only come when or if we
find the appropriate treatment for her condition (medication, surgery,
cure, or whatever).

When we believe our children's success is dependent on external
remedies, we're delivering our children's lives and their futures into
the hands of a society that will continue to marginalize them because
of their perceived imperfections and deficits. In addition, we're preparing for failure. For the "if" or the "when" may never happen....

What does it mean to unconditionally believe in your child and
his future? It means that, right now, regardless of your child's label
or the severity of his disability, you believe he will be successful
and will live the life of his dreams.... Many of us have a generalized
attitude that, "I'll believe it when I see it." But when it comes to our
children, we must adopt the attitude, "I'll see it when I believe it."[7]

When we accept disability as natural, we think differently and
behave differently. As parents, we begin to treat our children differently. We don't see them as a collection of body parts that need
improvement; we see them, sometimes for the first time, as whole
beings. This causes us to rethink what's really important.[8]

---

6.   Confirmation is a sacrament in the Catholic Church. Generally young people receive
this sacrament in their teenage years, after two years of study and prayer.

7.   Kathie Snow, *Disability Is Natural* (Woodland Park, Colorado: BraveHeart Press,
2001), 229.

8.   Ibid., 231.

[The] Congress [of the United States] finds that

> disability is a natural part of the human experience that does not diminish the right of individuals with developmental disabilities to live independently, to exert control and choice over their own lives, and to fully participate in and contribute to their communities through full integration and inclusion in the economic, political, social, cultural, and educational mainstream of United States society.[9]

Your child may have significant disabilities, but what abilities might he or she have?

- The ability to love and be loved.
- A strong will to live and succeed like all children.
- An inviting innocence.
- The ability to make others stop taking life for granted.
- A simple peace in body and spirit.
- The grace to bring families and friends together.

Parenting a child with difficulties is a journey and an adventure, mostly mundane, frequently jarring, sometimes sad, and occasionally mystical. All such journeys begin with a dream. And so does this one.

The Dream Child

Every parent has dreams. You might imagine that your child will become a great missionary, doctor, lawyer, parent, sports figure, journalist, educator, author, manager, entrepreneur, or cook. Your child, however, may have entirely different dreams, talents, and interests. Most parents have to modify their hopes for their children.

> Our world came crashing down in a matter of minutes. Our baby was no longer our baby. Instead, in the medical community, she became a "fetus with a fatal defect."
>
> *(Christine, mom of Grace Ann who*
> *was born with Trisomy 18)*

These are the children that mothers do not "dream" about, yet these are their greatest gifts, beyond what we could ever dream. These are the children who will transform many lives.

> *(Doreen, mom of Gianna who was born*
> *with Trisomy 13 and holoprosencephaly)*

---

9. *The Developmental Disabilities Assistance and Bill of Rights Act of 2000* (42 USC 15001 SEC. 101. FINDINGS, PURPOSES, AND POLICY) (Washington, DC: U.S. Department of Health and Human Services), (a) (1).

The child of your dreams is not the child you conceived. Your child, however, knows nothing about your dreams. She does not feel sick, incapable, or hopeless. Nor does she know anything about diagnoses or predictions. She is happily tumbling and kicking, achieving what is normal for her and developing her unique abilities.

The key to good parenting is to crawl inside your children's skin and see the world through their eyes. Then you will strive to have their dreams, not yours, come true. Your unborn child has goals. She is to be warm, comfortable, and playful. When your child is born, the goals will change to being held, caressed, fed, changed, burped, and walked with. If your child lives, his goals will change. He will have certain dreams when he is ready. She will reach certain milestones on her own schedule. Help your child to become all that he or she can become. That is the goal, the journey, and the gift.

> I knew from the minute I saw her. And what once would have devastated me somehow changed me. This was MY baby, not some "retarded child" I was seeing on TV. I was not anguished about MY child with Down syndrome, but about the many children with Down syndrome who had mysteriously come through my life prior to her, small messengers whose presence I had never acknowledged. I was ashamed. I loved this baby without reservation. I was already learning about my own prejudices. I knew I had better start learning, and fast. I told everyone who would listen about the Down syndrome. I was so proud of this child, I actually surprised myself. She attends a regular preschool program, potty trained before she was three, and is a very independent little kid. She is funny and spirited, stubborn and witty. She whistles little songs all day long. She idolizes her big brother. She loves to draw, and at three can put all the details into a drawing of a face. She is rather amazing, but then she is mine so I see her with a touch of prejudice.

> *(Michelle, mom of Ciarra who*
> *was born with Down syndrome)*

Disguised Treasure

Prenatal testing has changed your life. You are on a journey on which many have walked before you and many will walk after. Each journey is a bit different, but all are alike in one way. If you follow your little one's lead, you will come to recognize your child's unique abilities. You will know the gift of your child.

Remember Aladdin's lamp, the magic beans, the frog prince? Aladdin was about to toss away an old lamp because it was tarnished and bent, but he rubbed it and out popped a magic genie. Jack traded the family

Celine was diagnosed in utero with hypoplastic right heart sydrome which was correctable through a series of surgeries.

cow for a handful of beans which his mom threw out the window in disgust. Overnight the beans grew into a beanstalk that reached to a giant's treasure trove above the clouds. The frog prince sought a princess to kiss him so that he could turn back into a handsome man. What do these fairy tales have to do with your baby? They remind us that the apparently worthless and ugly can be an avenue to immeasurable value.

Your baby is not a label, a diagnosis, a syndrome, or a condition. He is a magic lamp, an enchanted bean, a frog prince.

So how did I react when I heard the news of our son? Even though choosing to abort his life was never an option for me, I still had a choice to make: to see him as a burden, a problem, or to accept him already then as a gift. I cannot explain why, but at that crucial moment I knew that I would accept my son just as he was intended to be. I responded with the words, "We would welcome such a child." I felt completely at peace, and in a sense almost honored at being given this child who would be truly "special."

(Edad, dad of Benjamin who was born with Down syndrome)

When Nathan was first diagnosed the blow was incredible. Because this is a fatal disease, there was that aspect to deal with, along with the fact that he would not be able to walk or talk or go through any of the developmental milestones other children do. I was in what felt like a gray fog for several months. I just went through the motions of life. I was very sleep-deprived because Nathan wasn't sleeping, plus I was grieving for my son. I do remember one day suddenly realizing time was ticking by. I wasn't enjoying my sweet baby, nor Emilie or my husband — I was just marking time. This isn't how I wanted to live my life, nor how I wanted to spend the precious little time Nathan probably had on earth. I wanted to enjoy every moment. So one day I just woke up and started living life again. I figured the thing to do was to fight his many illnesses and make the most of whatever time we had, giving him absolutely the best life we could.

(Jennifer, mom of Nathan who
was born with Menke's Disease)

If you can view your child as a treasure in disguise, the time of waiting for your baby's birth will change from a time of dread to time of joy. You will embrace the wonder of your child alive within you, and you will be able to face the future with hope.

The decision to carry my Joyann to term was a process, honestly. I knew that once she was out, if I changed my mind, there was no putting her back. I decided to go the natural way, let Joyann decide the day she would be born. As the weeks flew by, I was really glad I had decided to carry Joyann to term. The women on the internet [*who had also carried to term*] were so loving and helpful and understanding. I also read a lot, wanting to know everything I possibly could about anencephaly Finally the day to meet Joyann arrived after nearly five months of waiting!

(Jewell, mom of Joyann who
was born with anencephaly)

My pregnancy was hard both emotionally and physically, but each kick from this little life showed me it was worth it. I felt this was the only time I was going to have with this child so I was going to enjoy it as much as possible.

(Sue, mom of Lucas Adam who
was born with anencephaly)

Who to Tell

We live with our choices. Women who end their pregnancies find that those who urged them to do so are generally nowhere to be found support-wise months and years later. On the other hand, those who bring their babies to term have the support of family and friends, through the years.

We decided to tell everyone at church and at work, thinking there would be less awkwardness if we were open about it. We did it mainly via email and by telling a few people whom we asked to tell others. That let everyone know. We also told people not to be afraid to talk to us. The response was overwhelming. The people who shared hugs, tears, words of support, and prayers were invaluable to us. For the most part, we were able to talk with everyone very matter-of-factly. Many people commented about how "strong" we were. We knew that it was because of all the prayers on our behalf and the peace, comfort, and strength provided by God. We trusted that God would comfort us and help us through this so that we could some day join our daughter in heaven.

(Mindy, mom of Abigail who
was born with Trisomy 18)

Choose your confidants carefully. You deserve supportive friends.

Through the mothers' ministry at my church, I discovered the friendship possible between women who love the Lord. We truly are sisters in Him. My fourth child was conceived the same month that the mothers' ministry began. At twenty weeks, the doctors informed us that Clare Catherine had a severe birth defect, which would make it impossible for her to survive for more than a few minutes outside of my womb. My husband and I were devastated with grief. What would I say to people when they asked about my baby? How would she be received? Would people begin to avoid me, or avoid mentioning my pregnancy? I was afraid that I would end up alone in my suffering. But I decided that I would speak openly about her, that I would rejoice in her as a beloved child of God, and that I would make the most of the brief time I had been given to cherish her. What a miracle awaited us! My sisters in Christ fell in love with Clare, too! They entered fully with me into the joy of life and the pain of death. They would pat my belly and ask, "How's our Clare today?" with smiles on their faces and tears in their eyes. They even organized a baby shower to celebrate Clare's life, and I have never received more heartfelt gifts. My sister SueAnn gave Clare a velvet gown with matching dress shoes, saying, "Every girl should have a party dress." Jeannine and Therese found a haloed silver dove to represent her patron saint, Clare of Assisi. I received many picture frames and photo albums and from Ann, a little baby pink rosary that Clare later held at her funeral. Mirna wrapped up a big box of diapers, saying, "I believe in miracles, and I'm praying for one for you."

(Elizabeth, mom of Clare Catherine
who was born with anencephaly)

2

TESTS AND TERMINATIONS

God never shuts one door but he opens another.[1]

Irish Proverb

Remembering Tanner

I'm sitting here remembering your beautiful face
And longing to hold you once more.
My love for you will never cease;
It's you that I'll always adore.

My child, please know that I miss you so much
And the pain inside me still grows.
Our time together was way too short;
The reason, only the good Lord knows.

I know that you're now in Paradise
And yes, that brings me great joy.
But I'm your mom and it's hard to let go
Because you still are my little boy.

So pray for me, son, for my heart to mend
For it always will be filled with sorrow.
Time does not diminish my love for you;
I'll miss you yesterday, today, and tomorrow.

Renee Pierson, mom of Tanner who
was born with posterior urethral valves

Prenatal testing is both a blessing and a burden. A blessing because knowing that your baby has difficulties can help you plan ahead. A burden because of pressure to "decide."

Why Screen All Pregnant Women?

The Genetics Center, which offers "straightforward answers to common questions" via the internet, has this question and answer:

Why screen all pregnant women?

---

1. http://www.intuitionmission.com/wisdom_says.htm.

During a pregnancy, every couple is concerned about whether their baby will be healthy. Fortunately, over 95 percent of babies will not have any significant health or learning problems. Two relatively common disorders, Down syndrome and spina bifida, most often occur where there is no family history of these disorders. Since they are both serious conditions that can be prenatally diagnosed in the early stages of pregnancy, screening can be very helpful for any pregnant woman.[2]

The site goes on to discuss what will happen if the test results are abnormal.

If an abnormal screening result is obtained, a couple may be asked to consult a geneticist, who will obtain a detailed family and pregnancy history, review the results of the screening tests, and help the couple and the obstetrician decide how to proceed with further testing.[3]

The information sounds innocuous. However, an "abnormal screening result" may prompt a doctor or geneticist to advocate pregnancy termination.

Based on the level two ultrasound, the doctor felt certain that our baby had Trisomy. He was insistent that I have an amnio to confirm the diagnosis. At first I resisted due to the risks involved with amniocentesis, but the doctor pushed me to have it done, to definitively rule out Trisomy. I was sent to a genetic counselor who told us all the horrible things Trisomy babies deal with. He strongly encouraged us to terminate. Even if the baby lived, he would have all these complications. When we told him he would not terminate, he said that they could not help us and we were on our own.

(Sandy, mom of Casey who was born with Trisomy 18)

The perinatologist, who was somewhat sympathetic, asked us, "What did we want to do?" and offered her help. A bit confused, I asked her what she meant. Well, of course, "Did we want to terminate?"

(Doreen, mom of Gianna who was born with Trisomy 13 and holoprosencephaly)

---

2. The Genetics Center, Inc. (Smithtown, New York), http://www.thegeneticscenter.com/serumscr.htm.

3. Ibid.

The attending physician sent us to the genetics counselor. The counselor emphasized how horrible and fatal the condition was. We told her that termination was not an option. I asked her if she had any support for me. She said she would get back to me and give me the name of someone who had a child like this. I am still waiting.

(Christine, mom of Grace Ann who
was born with Trisomy 18)

Every single one of the doctors came up with same diagnosis of Potter's Syndrome and they all recommended that we terminate the pregnancy.

(Donna, mom of Jonathan who
was born with Potter's Syndrome)

Certain tests are accurate only if the exact time of conception is known.

Michael researched the triple screening test and learned that the results were only accurate if the blood test is given knowing the actual weeks of gestation. There was no way my doctor knew the actual gestation of our baby. Yet she informed me in a very matter-of-fact way that we had a problem. I think of parents who rely on the results of the triple blood screen tests and trust their doctor's advice to consider aborting their baby. They don't realize that the tests are reliable for detecting healthy babies but unreliable for detecting abnormalities. Too many women have relied on the test results and aborted what they thought was a baby with an abnormality only to learn afterwards that the baby did not have any abnormality. Not to mention that the message being sent to society is that people with disabilities should be eliminated and that parents should be spared from raising these children. Why can't we just accept people the way they are, with their differences?

(Lisa, mom of Brady who
was born without any disability)

Additional Tests

If first tests indicate a problem, doctors will schedule additional tests. Some mothers refuse these.

My doctor said there was a problem with the baby's bowel. He wanted me to undergo an anmiocentesis and I refused. It became a battle of the wills. If I had the amnio, the doctors would have discovered Joey's Trisomy 18 and they would have pressured me to abort. I wanted to avoid that pressure.

(Erin, mom of Joey who
was born with Trisomy 18)

I remember refusing the alpha-fetoprotein test, saying, "No. That would just give me one more thing to worry about." The nurse kept pushing the test at us. Finally, my husband blurted out our religious beliefs and said we wouldn't terminate even if something was wrong with our child. The nurse then said, "Oh, so you'll take whatever God sends you?" and we said "Yeah," then left, a little annoyed.

(Jewell, mom of Joyann who
was born with anencephaly)

By seven months, I had preeclampsia. The baby was measuring small. The following month the doctor sent me to a geneticist. The geneticist suspected Trisomy 18. I was thirty weeks pregnant. My doctor began to monitor Maria with a continuous sonogram and to treat my preeclampsia with bed rest. The geneticist informed me of the perils of Trisomy 18. She and my OB were persistent in trying to persuade me to have amniocentesis to positively identify the baby's genetic disorder. It was suggested to me that positive identification would lead to induction of labor and subsequent birth. I knew this would kill her. Since I had recently reread the Holy Father's encyclical on the vocation and dignity of women,[4] the significance of the dignity of the human person was fresh in my mind. To allow them to determine the diagnosis of Trisomy 18 positively would be a direct assault against the baby's dignity as a person. My husband and I chose to make the doctors go blind — to treat me for preeclampsia and allow God to bring Maria to birth in His time.

(Jeanne, mom of Maria G. who
was born with Trisomy 18)

Amniocentesis comes with a risk of miscarriage. Some parents do not want to take that risk.

As for Emmil, we didn't know through the whole pregnancy whether or not he had Down syndrome. We did NOT get any further testing. The doctor told me to get the test just so I would know for sure to alleviate stress. I knew that there was a risk of miscarriage and I wasn't about to risk that AT ALL.

(Ashli, mom of Emmil who was born without Down syndrome)

Doctors often assume that parents choose follow-up tests in order to terminate if a serious problem is confirmed.

As no therapeutic intervention yet exists to cure D[own] s[yndrome] [or most other prenatally diagnosed conditions] or ameliorate some of its manifestations in utero, prenatal screening and diagnosing have

---

4. John Paul II, "Mulieris Dignitatem" ("On the Dignity and Vocation of Women"), 15 August 1988, http://www.vatican.va/holy_father/john_paul_ii/apost_letters/documents/hf_jp-ii_apl_15081988_mulieris-dignitatem_en.html.

almost exclusively existed to allow women the option of terminating their pregnancies. Knowing this, health care providers have historically operated under the assumption that if a woman consents to prenatal screening or diagnosing, she must believe that having a child with DS [or another prenatally diagnosed condition] would be an undesired outcome and wish to terminate her pregnancy if such a diagnosis were made prenatally. The results of this study indicate that this is not true for all women. Consequently, health care providers should appreciate that many women consent to prenatal testing with ambivalence or no intent whatsoever to terminate.[5]

My husband and I thought our son had Down syndrome because of what a perinatologist told us at a twenty-week appointment. The nuchal fold was chubby, and he said that only 1 percent of the children he saw with our son's measurement DIDN'T have DS, meaning 99 percent did. "Go ahead and get an amnio today so you can take care of it as soon as possible," he said. I think he was a little disappointed when I told him I'd let him take my arms and legs before I'd let him take my child.

(Ashli, mom of Emmil who
was born without Down syndrome)

How Information Is Presented

We generally trust the medical community to present factual, unbiased information. However, the presenter's personal bias may color the way information is presented. The doctor who supported Christine in bringing her seriously ill daughter Grace Ann to birth noted:

There's definitely a feeling out there that a life like this is not worth pursuing to the end of the pregnancy. I don't know how we've come to this end, but we have. A large portion of the obstetrics community believes these lives are less worthy, in the sense that babies that appear to be normal are, in a sense, more worthy.... You can speculate on the reasons as much as I can. Is it abortion on demand? Even the March of Dimes's healthy baby program — the March of Dimes does a tremendous amount of good work. But the promotion is based on identifying and eliminating unhealthy babies. Somewhere, we have developed a definition of healthy and, in pursuit of "healthy," there are babies deemed unhealthy. Their moms are strongly steered toward termination.[6]

5. Brian G. Skotko, "Prenatally diagnosed Down syndrome: Mothers who continued their pregnancies evaluate their health care providers," *American Journal of Obstetrics and Gynecology* 192 (2005): 675.

6. Dr. John Wagner, "Witness to Love: The Short, Beautiful and Inspiring Life of Grace Ann Nugent," *National Catholic Register*, 5–11 January 2003: 17.

I anxiously asked him what the treatment was, and he matter-of-factly said, "There is no treatment; you must terminate." My doctor made an appointment for a more detailed sonogram. The radiologist also recommended that we terminate. We saw several other specialists, including perinatologists. Every single one came up with the same diagnosis of Potter's Syndrome and they all recommended that we terminate the pregnancy.

(Donna, mom of Jonathan who
was born with Potter's Syndrome)

Two prominent obstetricians recognize that:

Termination of pregnancy has become the de facto management of choice for lethal fetal conditions, and health care providers as a group may be more favorably disposed to this method of management than either the general public or the pregnant woman herself. Others have speculated, and our own experience has suggested, that if a specific model of prenatal care for these patients is instituted and explicitly presented as an option, the number of patients choosing this form of management may increase. Therefore, some providers may question the wisdom of committing resources to an approach possibly encouraging what they perceive as a "less than optimal" parental choice.[7]

In simpler words, most of the medical community believes that the best way to deal with "lethal fetal conditions" is termination of the pregnancy. The same might be said for other conditions that are not fatal or not immediately fatal. These include Down syndrome, sickle cell anemia, cystic fibrosis, muscular dystrophy, limb differences, hydrocephalus, and any number of conditions involving correctable organ defects. For example, 90 percent of babies who are diagnosed in utero with Down syndrome are aborted[8] even though Down syndrome is not a fatal condition.

Obstetricians often have little direct contact during their training with children who have developmental disabilities. Physicians often distance themselves from their own personal beliefs in a commitment to provide balanced information for the new mother. A survey of 499 primary care physicians revealed that 63% reported that they "tried to be as unbiased as possible about delivering a prenatal diagnosis." Thirteen percent reported that they "emphasize" the negative aspects of D[own] S[yndrome] so that parents would favor a termination, 10% actively "urge" parents to terminate, and 10% indicated that they

---

7. Drs. Nathan J. Hoeldtke and Byron C. Calhoun, "Perinatal Hospice," *American Journal of Obstetrics and Gynecology* 185 (2001): 528.

8. Trudy Johnson, "When a Pregnancy Test Shows Down Syndrome" (Focus on the Family Ireland, 2006), http://www.family.ie/marriage/downs.html.

"emphasize" the positive aspects of DS so that parents favor continuation and 4% actively "urge" parents to continue the pregnancy.[9]

Look at these statistics again. Twenty-three percent of obstetricians interviewed purposely present a diagnosis of Down syndrome in a negative light, so that the parents will "choose" to terminate. That is one doctor out of four. Your doctor may be that one.

Prevention

The emphasis on "preventing" illness or congenital disabilities has come to mean preventing people who have these conditions. Kathie Snow, mother of a child with cerebral palsy, warns, "Do not let a disability label or a doctor's prognosis convince you that your child needs to be changed. She doesn't need to change or be changed; society needs to change. Your child is fine just the way she is. *Your child is perfect.* If you don't believe that, change the way you think! Change your definition of perfect; don't try to change your child. Either all of us are perfect or none of us are."[10]

"Your belief in your child and his potential has a greater influence over his success than his disability."[11] We obtain medical care and services, not to "fix" our children, but to help them realize their potential.

> To be a mother of a child with a disability is not for sissies, but there is good news — it will change you. I wondered if I could be a good mom. Could I actually cope with all of the doctors, the trips to the emergency room, the surgeries, the testing? There were times when I didn't think I could. I did. This was my son, my flesh, a blessing, an opportunity to raise a child that I had borne to love and to cherish. I assumed I would do all of the teaching, but this young man has taught me how to continue to be a good and better person altogether. I owe this to my son, who, twelve years ago, was born with such a dismal prognosis that it seemed like his life would not be worth living. A life that could not possibly be of any benefit to himself or others, a life that, without given the chance, would have been lost and what a much emptier place this world would be.
>
> *(Ashley, mom of Nick who*
> *was born with spina bifida)*

---

9. Brian G. Skotko, "Prenatally diagnosed Down syndrome: Mothers who continued their pregnancies evaluate their health care providers," *American Journal of Obstetrics and Gynecology* 192 (2005): 670–71.

10. Snow, 63.

11. Ibid., 64.

Differences in Perception

Doctors tend to see babies as clinical diagnoses while mothers tend to see them with love.

> When I was twenty years old, I, although pregnant, left my abusive boyfriend. When I went to the doctor, the health care workers said things like, "What do you plan to do about this pregnancy?" In my mind there was only one thing I could do — have a baby. In the sixth month of pregnancy I had my first ultrasound. I'll never forget the words. "Your baby has an abnormality in the brain." At my next OB appointment a woman doctor proceeded to explain that I would be better off if I terminated the pregnancy. She told me my baby would be retarded, and that a termination would be best for him. His condition was called hydrocephalus [fluid on the brain]. I was determined to have this baby even if the whole world was against it! Another doctor recommended that I have labor induced at thirty-two weeks, so that a shunt could be put in his brain to drain off some fluid. I told God that I would love my little boy and accept him no matter what. God did give me a healthy baby; the surgery was never needed. Although he still has hydrocephalus, it has caused no problems. Dylan is almost nine years old now, and how I would love to take him to the doctors and show them the little boy the world would be "better off without."
>
> *(Shellie, Dylan's mom)*

Widely used by doctors, *The Catalog of Prenatally Diagnosed Conditions*[12] lists over eight hundred conditions that can be diagnosed in utero. The text also details how to make the diagnosis. Compare this clinical description of a terminated "fetus" diagnosed in utero with "urethral obstruction malformation sequence," which includes "posterior urethral valves," with a mother's description of her son with the same condition:

> The fetus reported by Nevin and associates (1983b) also had distention of the bladder, abdomen, and ureters, and hydronephrosis; diagnosis of Trisomy 18 was made. After termination and an autopsy, the fetus was found to have double-outlet right ventricle with an overriding aorta, ventricular septal defect, and hypoplastic left atrium and ventricle. There was no neural tube defect present.[13]

---

12.   David D. Weaver, with the assistance of Ira K. Brandt, *The Catalog of Prenatally Diagnosed Conditions, 3rd ed.* (Baltimore, Maryland: The John Hopkins University Press, 1999 with periodic updates).

13.   Ibid., 180–81.

At the perinatologist's office, our son was diagnosed with a rare condition called posterior urethral valves (PUV). The perinatologist also suspected either Down syndrome, Trisomy 13, or Trisomy 18. It was suggested that we terminate the pregnancy. We decided to seek treatment options. In my thirty-third week of pregnancy, I went into early labor and had to deliver our son via emergency cesarean section. A team of pediatricians began working right away on our six-pound-fourteen-ounce precious little Tanner. Tanner had only one very under-developed lung that would not be able to support life. This was a direct result of the PUV. We spent the next thirty-six hours holding Tanner and loving him. Although I knew my son was dying, I had never been happier in my whole life because he was the greatest gift I had ever received. I would do it all over again just for those wonderful thirty-six hours that we had with Tanner.

(Renee, Tanner's mom)

Here is another description from *The Catalog of Prenatally Diagnosed Conditions* and then a mother's thoughts on her child born with the same condition:

Holoprosencephaly (Includes Aproscenephaly; Cebocephaly; Cheilognathopalatoschisis; Cyclopia; Ethmocephaly) … Aprosencephaly …. The infant reported by Reynolds and Waldstein (1989) had micro-cephalus, a bony defect of the calvarium in the center of the forehead, a diamond-shaped opening in midface, a single fused ocular structure, absence of the nose, small philtrum and mouth, and absence of the premaxilla. At autopsy the cerebral hemispheres were absent and replaced by separate cystic structures, the prosencephalon was repre-sented by an ovoid mass, and there was absence of the crista galli, crib-riform plate, and the first, second, fourth, and sixth cranial nerves.[14]

I will never forget my Gianna moving and growing inside of me. I loved her so much. I knew that her birth would bring her death and I did not want to say goodbye. I prayed for three things: for acceptance of God's will, for great good to result from her life; and that she would have a nose (because of the holoprosencephaly, she was sup-posed to have a large cleft between her eyes and an open hole where her nose would be). Praise be to God, she was born with a nose and my children were able to meet her and we have pictures hanging on our wall of her. I also know that a great good came from this. She has already affected many lives. She has had so much impact on me. God is transforming me. Every day I pray that God will guide me. For the

---

14.   Ibid., 96–97.

first time in my life, I am truly listening to His call and have my ears
and heart awaiting His direction.

(Doreen, mother of Gianna who was born
with Trisomy 13 and holoprosencephaly)

Doctors are capable of considering as "worthless" even "normal"
babies who are unwanted by their parents:

We had a twenty-four-week gestation baby born today. Mom came
into the emergency room with pain early on, wouldn't answer questions of gestational age since little prenatal care. Baby born early
afternoon. Good MD took right to warmer. Spontaneous cry, (little
boy), only needed oxygen, no CPR. When Pedi NICU Docs arrived,
were told Mom didn't want baby. But this attending MD said, "I have
a patient here, and he's good. I think we need to go forward." So,
despite the fact that one fellow in OB reminded us all Mom hadn't
wanted baby right now, we did everything.

(Judy, an ob-gyn nurse)

If a doctor is willing to forego treatment for a premature but healthy,
yet "unwanted" baby, what might be the response if the baby has a serious health issue?

Euphemisms

A euphemism is "the substitution of an agreeable or inoffensive expression for one that may offend or may suggest something unpleasant."[15]
Those who deal with serious prenatal diagnoses often use them. Terms
that refer to pregnancy and birth are used to name the processes of abortion. This makes abortion sound like birth.[16]

We were given two choices: we could terminate or we could continue the pregnancy. Most women terminate. "Could you, my doctor,
do the termination?" "No, you would have to go to the Women's
Center." "But that is an abortion clinic!" I finally understood.
Termination was abortion! In my shocked mind I had not understood
that! I need to hold my baby not have it torn apart in pieces! "In that
case we can induce labor but would have to inject a solution into the
baby's heart to stop it before inducing." I can't do that! That would
cause my baby to die!

(Sue, mom of Lucas Adam who
was born with anencephaly)

---

15. *Merriam-Webster Online Dictionary*, http://m-w.com/dictionary/euphemism.

16. Melinda Tankard Reist, *Defiant Birth: Women Who Resist Medical Eugenics* (North
Melbourne, Victoria: Spinifex, 2006): 11.

Medical professionals may try to assure you that the termination procedure is not an abortion. It is merely "bringing on the birth." Doctors may talk about "early delivery" of your child, "medical induction of labor," "interrupting your pregnancy," or "ending the pregnancy early." They may tell you that your baby will be "stillborn."

Is your doctor suggesting birth or abortion?

Birth means bringing a living child into the world to live as long as possible. Abortion means bringing a dead child into the world or, if the child survives the abortion, to hasten death either with nontreatment or active euthanasia. Ask your doctor:

- ❧ Is my baby alive now? If so, will he or she be stillborn after this procedure?

- ❧ Will this procedure help my baby to be born alive with the maximum chance of long-term survival?

- ❧ Will this procedure cause my baby to be born dead or dying, unable to survive?

- ❧ Will doctors be available to help my baby survive?

- ❧ Are you suggesting this procedure so that I can confront my baby's death as soon as possible (say goodbye early)?

If you want to maximize your baby's chances of survival, remain pregnant as long as is safely possible.

> The level two ultrasound showed that my baby did have anencephaly. Technicians said my baby wasn't "really alive"; she was only able to live through circulation in the umbilical cord. I asked, "How can she move and kick then???" They said it was all due to the circulation, and that made no sense to me. They likened me to her life support. I thought of patients on life support, lying motionless, out of it. That isn't my baby! She moves at will and is very much alive. Joyann would punch out on my stomach, and my husband would push in that spot, then she'd go "bam bam" real hard back in the same spot. Seems to me, if it was all random, sporadic movements, the baby wouldn't be able to move in very controlled movements like that. I feel the doctors just want to "dehumanize" our babies, so they can justify ending their lives. The perinatal center offered a D&C, saying one doctor "may be able to pull the baby out in one piece." I said, "Certainly not!" They then talked about induction, of giving birth to the baby after they medically induce labor. I thought it sounded better than abortion. I gave them permission to see if my insurance company would cover the procedure. A few days later, I got a phone call saying it was arranged for me to deliver my baby! I said, "I'm not ready yet!" They pushed me, saying, "It has to be done before twenty-four weeks." I said, "The perinatal center said I could be induced at ANY time in my whole pregnancy."

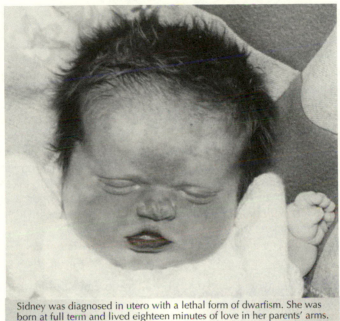

Sidney was diagnosed in utero with a lethal form of dwarfism. She was born at full term and lived eighteen minutes of love in her parents' arms.

"Well, the hospital won't do it past twenty-four weeks." It started to sound like termination to me.

(Jewell, mom of Joyann who was born with anencephaly)

Many parents want to continue a pregnancy while their medical team wants to end it. The parents think about the positive outcomes of giving birth while the "experts" paint a bleak picture. Parents are looking for support and information while doctors are pressuring them to decide quickly. Is it any wonder that many parents conclude that termination is a necessity?

[*We were pregnant with twins, one of whom had been diagnosed with anencephaly.*] The doctor did another ultrasound and confirmed what the other hospital had seen. He told us that the best thing was a selective reduction, which is injecting the sick baby with saline that will kill him. He didn't explain to us more options or ask us to think about it. We were in shock and scheduled the procedure for four days later. I remember sobbing and thinking that we were going to have to end our baby's life. My husband was inconsolable; we kept thinking back to the images on the monitor of the babies and their little hearts beating, but we thought that this had to be done to save the other twin's life. That Tuesday we went to the hospital. The nurse

brought the babies' images up and I started crying — I asked her
what the sex of the sick baby was and she told me, "A boy." Our son
— our beautiful son — we were never going to hold him or tell him
that we loved him. The other baby was a girl — our daughter — she
would never know her brother or play with him. The doctor could
see how distraught we were and he asked if we were sure we wanted
to go through with it. I looked at him puzzled and said, "We have
a choice?" He then explained that there was a possibility that both
babies would abort and that it is quite possible to carry both twins full
term but that the anencephalic baby would most likely be born dead
or die within minutes of being born. My husband and I agreed that it
was not up to us to make this decision — who were we to take the life
of our son — to not give him a chance? Miracles happen every day.
So we left with both our babies. As long as they were inside of me I
would make sure they were okay.

> *(Jennifer, mom of Emily, and of her twin brother Matthew*
> *who was born with anencephaly)*

Is your doctor saying that you MUST end this pregnancy? If so, ask why.

The Why of Testing and Termination

Doctors, geneticists, family members, clergy, and friends may suggest,
and even insist on, termination. The reasons are many, but each involves
a philosophy rather than a necessity:

❧ Termination to alleviate your suffering.

> The attitude of doctors seems to be that the woman can't handle an
> adverse diagnosis so they want to take it out of the woman's hands
> and they think she will thank God for their intervention. They don't
> give women any credit for being able to handle the baby. But if you
> have the baby, once the baby dies, you want to turn back the clock
> and have that child in your life again.
>
> *(Erin, mom of Joey who*
> *was born with Trisomy 18)*

❧ Termination so that you can forget about this baby and try again.

> She told me that my child's prospects of even being born alive were
> slim and that if he were born he would have no quality of life. She
> told me that there really were no alternatives. She told me that I was
> doing the right thing, and I could be pregnant again and have a healthy
> baby. She turned back around with an appointment book to schedule
> an abortion.
>
> *(Stephanie, mom of Chandler who was born*
> *without any disability)*

℞ Termination to preserve your physical stamina or mental health.

I also went to see a counselor as I was very worried about how the kids would handle me carrying to term. He advised me not to go through the pregnancy as I had a diagnosis of depression and he was worried about my mental and emotional health. What about my mental and emotional health if I had to live my life with the knowledge that I consented to kill one of my children? He said not to worry about the kids as they would adjust to whatever and would follow Doran's and my lead.

(Sue, mom of Lucas Adam who was
born with anencephaly)

℞ Termination because you cannot handle a child with significant needs.

My family thought I'd have a nervous breakdown, that carrying the pregnancy to term would destroy me. My family didn't think of me as someone that selfless. I think carrying to term is something most people would not do so they can't grasp why someone would do it. It really challenges their belief system, makes them ask how far are they willing to go. Andrew was born and he lived five days. He did not have nearly the amount of problems that doctors thought he would have. We were able to hold him and it was beautiful. He died on Easter and it was a gift, an incredible journey. I feel like the odds which the doctors gave me were manufactured. They tried to encourage me to end the pregnancy. Most of these babies will be born if given a chance even though they may not thrive. Doctors think that women can't handle it.

(Emily, mom of Andrew who
was born with Trisomy 13)

℞ Termination to keep your child's disability from harming your family.

They fear they cannot meet the needs of the child. I am nobody special. I had no experience with cancer when I had to learn to care for Alex who got leukemia. I have a little experience with some issues that Sidney may face, but know nothing about feeding tubes or breathing support. But I know I can learn. And I trust the doctors and nurses to teach me well before they send me home.

(Laura, mom of Sidney,
born with lethal dwarfism)

Another doctor, knowing what the Citarellas had decided, when Tito was not present, turned to Mimi and said, "Think of the burden you are placing on your other two children."[17]

---

17. "Fighting for Claire," 5.

༈ Termination to prevent your child from suffering.

They fear that the child will not have a good quality of life, and that their condition may cause them suffering, or that treating the condition may cause suffering. We did not want to subject Sidney to needless suffering. But pain that could give her life, or that would help her live better, would be worth it. Quality of life for babies is an issue of love. If they can give and receive love, then life is good for them. Babies who suffer but are loved, live because they choose to. I do not want my baby to suffer, but I do want her to live the life she is fighting to live. I want to make sure that while she fights, she is loved, held, and cared for. When she stops fighting, we will let her go.

(Laura, mom of Sidney who
was born with a lethal form of dwarfism)

༈ Termination so that you will not be "a bother" to others.

I told my obstetrician that we wanted to continue the pregnancy and give our child the best possible chance. He told me that we were taking the "harder road." I asked him three times if he would follow me for the duration of the pregnancy. (He had never had a patient willingly choose to continue a pregnancy with a fatal diagnosis.) He said that he would follow me, but I could sense some reluctance. I asked him for resources including support groups for women who choose to continue their pregnancies. He said, "There are no groups like that available." [*Note: The internet lists many such groups. See Appendix B of this book for a sampling.*] I asked for the name of another mom who had continued a pregnancy. He replied that he did not know any. I felt very alone.

(Donna, mom of Jonathan who
was born with Potter's Syndrome)

༈ Termination to lower hospital and insurance costs, which will be minimal if you terminate. If you give birth to a living baby who requires treatment, however, the costs could be very high.

The results of the blood test prompted the doctor to order an amniocentesis and ultrasound. It was fully paid for by the State of California, as would be the abortion. I was given a consultation, warning me of the risk for a woman my age giving birth to a child with a disability. This process was about Ben as a long-term expense to the state versus a short-term expense of an abortion. This would be the first of many experiences that would be a clear reflection of attitudes in the policies that guide the lives of people with disabilities and their families. My life's work would become a challenge to those attitudes.

(Terry, mom of Ben who
was born with multiple disabilities)

༈ Termination so that professionals can study your baby clinically.

Most of these babies are terminated. Doctors advise that parents terminate, then agree to an autopsy so they can "study the condition and learn more about it." They do NOT want the parents to continue the pregnancy and try to help the baby LIVE, which would certainly teach them MORE about the condition than dissection ever could. Such an attitude is unfortunately common.

(Laura, mom of Sidney who
was born with a lethal form of dwarfism)

↬ Termination of a "compromised" baby in a multiple pregnancy, so that the dying baby will not threaten the lives of the sibling(s). This fear is unfounded; this baby is no threat to the other(s).

The ultrasound was being made, first the baby at the right, then the baby at the left and then everything went silent. One baby had anencephaly. She would certainly die, either before if not soon after birth. In my thirty-second week of pregnancy, Anna and Tess were born. At first I was afraid to look at Anna, but she was beautiful. She lived four hours and will always be in our hearts. When we came back to the hospital after the funeral, we immediately went to our daughter Tess to hold her close and to share our grief. Tess is four years old now and a lovely child with a heart of gold. I am proud to be the mother of my two girls, and I believe that some day we will meet again.

(Tineke, mom of Anna and Tess)

↬ Termination to avoid a lawsuit. You cannot sue if you end the pregnancy because, even though others may have pressured you to terminate, ultimately the decision to do so is yours. If you proceed with the pregnancy and you feel that your baby was improperly treated, however, you could sue the physician, hospital, and/or other professionals for malpractice.

The routine ultrasound revealed that Andrew's brain and stomach were completely full of fluid. The doctor said, "It looks like the baby is compromised and has hydrocephalus." I already had two children with Down syndrome (our firstborn and then her brother whom we had adopted) and I wanted to continue the pregnancy. The doctor said, "The baby looks so compromised that it could affect your health. You need to get an amnio to be sure." The amnio revealed that the baby had Trisomy 13. The likelihood that he would make it full term was 10 percent. I was fine with those odds. I just wanted to nurture my baby and, if he didn't make it, I would honor his life in utero. All information from the doctors was really negative and disappointing. Our pediatrician was horrified. He saw "lawsuit" written all over this.

(Emily, mom of Andrew who
was born with Trisomy 13)

☙ Termination due to a utilitarian philosophy that every human being ought to have a minimal "quality of life" or "health." Many people believe that babies with significant health conditions require "too much money" and may never be able to "produce" or "be useful." One doctor termed this attitude "handiphobia," that is "fear of people with handicaps."[18]

Today I was reading an article about ethicist Dan W. Brock's lecture at the University of Rhode Island's tenth Honors Colloquium on November 19.[19] "Society might be better off if it prevents the birth of blind and severely disabled children." Blindness and severe cognitive dysfunction are two disabilities Brock would prevent. Ben was born deaf-blind. His cognitive and physical disabilities would gradually reveal themselves. According to Brock, "Preventing a severe disability is not for the sake of the child who will have it. Rather, it is for the sake of less suffering and loss of opportunity in the world." I see things from quite a different point of view.

(Terry, mom of Ben who
was born with multiple disabilities)

☙ Termination due to devaluing those with disabilities.

"Of course, no one wants to adopt a defective baby." This was said with much emotion (and not much charm) by an older gentleman in a class at a local university. Since I had told the story of my daughter Karen, born with Down syndrome and a severe heart defect, the pro-abortion students were extremely vocal about the personal and societal justifications for aborting a baby like Karen. Hence the statement about no one wanting to adopt a "defective" baby. "Happily, sir," I told the senior student, "you are wrong. Even back when I had Karen, I found out from the National Down Syndrome Association that there was a list of people waiting to adopt a baby with Down syndrome. Just last night," I added, "I found a new website for matching prospective parents with children who had chromosomal and physical defects." The student refused to believe that this could be true.

(Nancy, Karen's mom)

☙ Termination because of the belief that the baby has no soul, is not a person, or is not human yet.

---

18.   Dr. Carlo Bellieni, neonatologist, in his course "The Myth of the Perfect Child," given at the Regina Apostolorum Athenaeum's School of Bioethics. From a Zenit News Agency internet release, 16 December 2005. See http://vitalsignsblog.blogspot.com/2005_12_01_archive.html.

19.   See Julie Novak, "Geneticist: Abort the blind and disabled." (Kingston, Rhode Island: *Narragansett Times*, 20 November 2002). http://www.ilusa.com/News/113002abort_disabled.htm.

We remembered this passage from the book of Psalms. "You formed my inmost being; you knit me in my mother's womb. I praise you, so wonderfully you made me; wonderful are your works! My very self you knew; my bones were not hidden from you, when I was being made in secret, fashioned as in the depths of the earth. Your eyes foresaw my actions; in your book all are written down; my days were shaped, before one came to be. How precious to me are your designs, O God; how vast the sum of them!" (Psalm 139:13–17). We knew that God made Arianna just the way she is and that His ways are perfect.

(Stephen, dad of Arianna who was born with anencephaly)

᛫ Termination because of a lack of faith in God or a Higher Power.

The thought of abortion did cross our minds when we reached a low point, but that passed and we trusted that God knew what he was doing when He created this child.

(Patricia, mom of Jessica who was born with limb differences of both arms and both legs)

᛫ Termination to purge the gene pool of disabilities (medical eugenics).

[T]he specialist offered us an abortion. He asked us to think about whether we wanted to bring another dwarf baby into the world.[20]

One of Kay-Marie's doctors remarked to her, "Now you are a young lady and might be thinking about boyfriends. We would like you to set up an appointment for birth control counseling and genetic counseling because you don't want to bring another child like you into the world, do you?"

(Madeline, mom of Kay-Marie who was born with two lower limb differences)

᛫ Termination because the baby is going to die anyway.

Mother Teresa compared babies to flowers. Some bloom for a whole season, some bloom for a day. But would a gardener even think of pulling out his daylilies because they last such a short time?
(Mary Ann Kreitzer, President and Editor of Les Femmes, The Women of Truth, in an email to "Church Militant," 22 April 2007)

A consultation in Manhattan, after the Citarellas had repeatedly made clear that they would, under no conditions, abort their child, impelled the specialist to send Mimi's file back to her primary doctor with the note: "HOPELESS case. Patient must be informed." The genetics specialist explained to the heartbroken Mimi that, though

---

20. Leisa Whitaker, "I Wouldn't Swap Them for Anything," in *Defiant Birth: Women Who Resist Medical Eugenics*: 214.

she would doubtlessly find some doctors to tell her "the glass is half full," the reality was that, anything they did for her baby "would be like rearranging chairs on the Titanic." He then proceeded, with great "compassion" to take her hand and to assure her that he would get her "through this." The solution? Abortion.[21]

You may be so pressured to terminate that you may feel, as one mother did, that she was at the "epicenter of the culture of death." Exasperated, this mother blurted out to one technician, "What's going on here? Are you people Nazis or something?"[22]

In extreme cases, pressure to terminate your pregnancy may be so great that you may have to take legal action. Doctors were agreeable to Lori Vance ending her pregnancy once they diagnosed that her unborn daughter Donna Joy had serious brain defects, but Lori had to threaten a lawsuit before she could find a hospital who would deliver her baby.[23]

Negative Effects of Termination

Some parents terminate their pregnancies without remorse. Others have very different experiences.

> There is no more devastating experience in a woman's life than to have her child destroyed in her own womb. The loss will never go away. The fact of a deceased child is just as real to the mother who had her child aborted as it is to the mother who sacrificed to save the life of her child but who tearfully stands beside his grave. With one exception: the guilt of a mother who has aborted is overwhelming, and especially so when it has been denied.
>
> *(Joan, mother of an aborted child)*

If you terminate, you may be left with regrets and the nagging feeling that you did not do all you could have done for your child.

> Josephine had a heart defect and a rare chromosomal disorder. A genetic doctor explained that, if our child lived, many surgeries would be needed to correct muscular and skeletal problems. Our baby would be severely physically and mentally retarded. Her physical features would be distorted and deformed. I had never been so afraid. One of the doctors stated that we needed to discuss our options. I thought she was referring to what needed to be done at the time of delivery. She was actually speaking of abortion, or "terminating the

---

21. "Fighting for Claire," 5.

22. Ibid.

23. Liz Townsend, "God Still Has Work for Her to Do," *National Right to Life News* (May 2007): 18.

pregnancy." My mind was reeling. My first response was "no way." But somewhere between that moment and that evening, I had decided to kill my beloved child, my Josephine. At thirty-six weeks — nine months pregnant — I lay in a clinic while a doctor injected my baby's heart with something to stop it from beating. I then went into labor before I was supposed to, and the doctor had to inject my baby again in order to make certain that she would definitely be dead when she was delivered. It was the most selfish act I have ever committed, and I regret it every single day. I have come a long way since then. But I hurt so much. I still can hardly bring myself to speak to Josephine, my daughter in Heaven. I still cannot forgive myself for what I've done. Why didn't anyone tell me that I would carry around this guilt and sorrow? Why wasn't I informed that my "choice" would cost me so much, emotionally and physically? Why didn't anyone remind me that a sick baby needs her mother to care for her and love her?

(Francesca, Josephine's mom)

Your spouse may not be supportive initially of carrying your baby to term. It takes time to adjust.

My husband thought that I was out of my mind for two months. I had to go forward with or without his blessing. It was a very stressful time in our marriage. Eventually my husband became really, really supportive. He is so proud of Andrew and in love with him, and now he totally understands why we went through to birth.

(Emily, mom of Andrew who was born with Trisomy 13)

The news given by the doctor didn't leave me feeling anxious until the baby's father said, "We will have an abortion then. Life would be too hard for the baby." Today Ben's dad loves his son deeply, but the journey he is on is quite different than mine.

(Terry, mom of Ben who was born with multiple disabilities)

Fathers, too, can be adversely affected when they end their child's life.

We went for a sonogram at about twenty-three-and-a-half weeks. Emmanuelle was diagnosed with a brain anomaly which included seizures and clenched fists. I don't see clenched fists. I don't see seizures. All I see is the most precious beautiful profile of a little girl looking skyward, eyes bright and open, the most beautiful of my three children, with her hands in front of her as if she is praying. This is the image etched in my mind forever. I let the doctors kill my daughter via a huge needle, a shot to the heart through my wife's belly as she lay sedated. I sat nearby, quietly praying to the Lord,

"Save her soul." The doctor had taken a picture of Emmanuelle. I suppose it is a picture of her lying dead on the table. I have not looked at the picture. But I know exactly where it is. I will always know. The grief is unbearable sometimes. Does the fact that I murdered my daughter show on my face?

(Eric, Emmanuelle's dad)

Choosing to end your pregnancy early rather than allowing nature to take its course may also have adverse effects on your physical health and that of subsequent children. Induced termination of pregnancy before thirty-two weeks has been proven to increase the mother's risk of breast cancer as well as increasing the risk of premature delivery in future pregnancies. Premature newborns are at greater risk of cerebral palsy than those born at full term.[24]

Mistaken Diagnosis

Parents are led to believe that prenatal tests are accurate. But often they are not. A recent study (2000) of three hundred fetal autopsies confirmed the prenatal diagnosis of disability in 39 percent of the babies; 61 percent of the prenatal diagnoses were incorrect![25]

The diagnosis of encephalocele was confirmed, and a fear they heard over and over again was that, because the skull was open, "the brain will be spilling out of the head." Throughout the pregnancy, doctors couldn't find the baby's cerebellum, the section of the brain which controls fine motor skills. Up to nine doctors and technicians couldn't find the cerebellum.... The horrifying consequences of what was being advocated [*termination*] was made real to Mimi. Waiting in the reception area for her next appointment, she found herself consoling a woman who also had received an adverse diagnosis. The woman had been told that her baby had Down syndrome and an abortion was performed, only to discover that there had been a misdiagnosis and the baby had been perfectly healthy. As the medical saga proceeded, Mimi found herself going to Mass every day, receiving the Eucharist and begging the Lord to touch her child and heal her with a miracle.... They [*the parents*] surrounded themselves with friends and family who shared their conviction that their baby was a precious gift from God regardless of her medical condition, and who prayed for Mimi and Tito's strength and consolation throughout the ordeal.... Mimi went into early labor.... She delivered by C-section

24. Angela Lanfranchi, MD, FACS, and Joel Brind, PhD,"Breast Cancer: Risks and Prevention" (Poughkeepsie, New York: Breast Cancer Prevention Institute, 2005): 13.

25. Reist, 25.

a healthy baby girl, to everyone's amazement.... There was, at the base of Claire's head, a small sack that was surgically removed two months after her birth. Whether Claire's story is a miracle worked by God in the womb of her mother or whether the multitude of specialists simply got confused by the sight of the small sack and offered a severe misdiagnosis, we may never know. But Mimi and Tito Citarella know that they chose the good in the face of trial — loving and accepting their child regardless of any medical condition — and that will have eternal rewards.[26]

My pregnancy was rough; my boyfriend was not very supportive. Once I saw the ultrasound at eighteen weeks I was in love! Then my world came crumbling down. The baby I had thought of terminating months earlier, whom I had grown to love, would possibly be born with birth defects. My ultrasound showed a dark spot on the heart, enlarged kidneys and thickening of the neck, which are characteristics of Down syndrome. I was at greater risk because my uncle has Downs. They couldn't guarantee me a healthy baby without an amnio, which I refused, because of the miscarriage risk. I was told I could terminate up to twenty-three weeks if my baby was to be mentally impaired. My boyfriend and I decided to hope and pray for the best. Shane William was born, three days late and perfect.

(Bonnie, mom of Shane who
was born without Down syndrome)

In September of 2001, my whole world changed. The first blow was the terrorist strike on 9-11. I began to question the security that I had held so dear to my heart. In the weeks that followed, my doctor told me that I was pregnant. My husband and I were struck with disbelief. We had taken precautions. The early months of my pregnancy were grim. My husband lost his job. We were forced to survive on my income. My son, who was two, was diagnosed with a seizure disorder. We lost our medical insurance. My daughter was three. We finally found state funded agencies that would assist us in finding insurance. After enduring this struggle for three months, my husband found a new job and I went for my ultrasound alone. The ultrasound technician said that most likely the doctor had predicted the wrong due date. So I was scheduled to come back in two weeks. It appeared that my child was a good candidate for Down syndrome and that my child's stomach was outside of his body. I had miscarried my last child and the emotions of that time came rushing back. One week later they added the possibility of toxoplasmosis, and water on the brain. I couldn't understand why God would let this happen. I lost my daughter and now I was going

---

26. "Fighting for Claire," 5–6.

to lose my son. Even if I didn't lose him, how could I take care of him? I already had a child who took so much energy dealing with his disabilities. The genetic counselor recommended an abortion. I asked her, "How could I even consider killing my child based on a theory?" She suggested an amnio which would confirm any doubts. I asked why this would not be performed before recommending an abortion. She told me in cases such as mine there is little doubt so it is unnecessary, but they would do it if it eased my mind. I was also scheduled to see a pediatric cardiologist. The cardiologist found a hole in his heart that should close up by the time he was born, but couldn't tell us that for sure. We were offered information on the abortion process once again. When the amnio and blood tests results were in, the genetic counselor told me that the tests came back negative, but there were strands of genetic defects that are undetectable. I was to come back for further testing. Everything came back in our favor. The doctors ordered another ultrasound. The new diagnosis was dwarfism. I was scheduled for an induction (three weeks after the due date). My son was born five pounds, twelve ounces, nineteen inches. Chandler's head was swollen. His soft spot was enormous. The CAT scan came back fine. Now Chandler is eighteen months old. He has not only met his developmental goals, he has exceeded them. My child has no signs of any of the disabilities that were predicted for him.

(Stephanie, mom of Chandler who
was born without any disability)

Consider prenatal test results to be "possibly correct." Accepting the diagnosis enables you to make plans for the future.

3

DEALING WITH DOCTORS

If you do not hope, you will not find what is beyond your hope.[1]

Clement of Alexandria

You Were Worth It All

You were our first child and it was so very exciting
When we found out that you would soon be arriving.
There was much work to do
To get ready for you
And we thanked the Lord for His wonderful blessing.

But when the day came for the ultrasound
We found that our whole world turned upside down.
Some said we should terminate
And not leave it up to fate.
They thought we could just bury the past in the ground.

But we were determined to do all that we could
Because being your parents we felt that we should.
There were many amnio-infusions
And two in-utero operations.
Whatever we could do to help you we would.

Finally the day came when you were born,
But when you arrived the doctors looked forlorn.
We didn't hear you cry.
Our minds went awry
And we felt like our hearts had been shattered and torn.

They whisked you away before we saw you.
They told us that they would do all they could do.
We prayed to our God,
Our strength and our rod,
For the fear that we felt we never before knew.

Soon they took us to see you in NICU
And our hearts overflowed at the sight of you.

---

1. http://www.aspiesforfreedom.com/showthread.php?tid=1664.

In our eyes you were perfect.
You definitely were worth it,
And we got to spend 36 wonderful hours with you.

Now that you are gone we have no regrets,
Just happy memories we'll never forget.
We're proud you're our son,
But your job here is done.
We'll be together again soon but not just yet.

> *Renee Pierson, mom of Tanner who*
> *was born with posterior urethral valves*

One mother of a child with severe difficulties noted that every parent of such a child is a pioneer. Every parent is striking out into uncharted territory and discovering things others have not discovered about children with their condition. You must become your child's advocate.

Your doctor and medical team are crucial, but they are human and, therefore, imperfect. Some doctors have difficulty seeing patients as individuals, families as unique units, and babies with difficulties as worthwhile humans. They may view you as a "case" rather than a person, thus distancing themselves from you. They want successful outcomes but may consider them impossible in your baby's regard. "Underneath it all, people are primarily afraid of failing. Professionals are not so different from you and me. We're all afraid of the unknown; we're all afraid of failing. Most of us try to avoid situations in which we might be uncomfortable or unsuccessful."[2]

> Then, after moving, I had to find a new OB doctor. None of the doctors would accept me as a patient since my baby had anencephaly. They said I'd have to go to a perinatologist in a nearby city. I didn't want to drive all that way. I didn't even have a babysitter for my son. Then in the phone book I found another practice that said "high risk" and called them. They accepted me right away and I found a wonderful doctor. I'm so thankful to God that I found him.
>
> *(Mary Sue, mom of Luke Daniel who*
> *was born with anencephaly)*

Tape Recorder

Take along a tape recorder when you visit your doctor. Tape recording often encourages a doctor to stick to the facts. You can listen to the words over and over, to process them fully and make clearer decisions. If your doctor refuses to allow the consultation to be recorded, find a new doctor!

---

2.   Snow, 74.

Statistics

Parents are often given statistics and probabilities. Here are some questions to help make sense of these:

- How accurate are these statistics?
- Is this information based on current data?
- Do these numbers pertain to MY child's exact condition?
- What are the numbers based upon?
- How many individuals were in the study?
- Are these statistics for THIS specific hospital and doctor?
- What is the experience of the entire team?
- What is the timeline of the statistics?
- Are we talking about survival in the hospital or after discharge?
- Who are the top three to five experts in this field? How can I find their studies and contact them?
- Who is giving me this information and what motivations might he or she have?
- How is the information being presented?
- How often is this condition incorrectly diagnosed?
- Is amniocentesis necessary? Will the results change the treatment options? What are the risks to my baby?
- What would you, as a doctor, do if this were your child? On what factual information, beliefs, ethical views, professional and personal experience do you base your view? Have you ever personally faced this dilemma?[3]

If you are told that the pregnancy could become life-threatening, ask the following questions and tape-record the responses:

- What do you mean by "endanger my life"?
- What proof do you have that continuing the pregnancy will or could be dangerous?
- How mild might this condition be? How severe?
- What are the life conditions?
- What are my chances, in percentages, of developing each problem? In other words, please tell me that there is a ____ percent chance of my developing this condition if I continue.

---

3. Some information on dealing with statistics is condensed from "Life and Death Decisions" by Debbie Hilton-Kamm, www.benotafraid.net/article.asp?id=19. Debbie's son Braedon was born with hypoplastic left heart syndrome.

- ✤ On what do you base the information and percentages?
- ✤ What would be the signs that the condition you describe is developing?
- ✤ What would be the signs that this condition has become life-threatening?
- ✤ What are my options if the pregnancy does become life-threatening?
- ✤ What is the danger to me of waiting to see if this pregnancy will or will not actually bring me to the brink of death?

Walter and I felt my doctor was just "going through the motions." We did not feel that he really understood what we were doing. And we also felt that he may have been concerned about his own liability. We reassured him that we would not sue him, that we wanted to give our baby the best chance and that we wanted to have a little time together to collect memories. He softened to some degree, but he just did not seem to fully "get it." He told us that our baby may not survive childbirth, and he told us "I do not want to do a C-section on you because you already know the outcome. I'm also concerned about the medical risk to you." After many, many conversations with him and prayers and support from those at hospice, we chose a C-section if our baby's life was in danger. We wanted to do everything we would have done for our other children. We let my doctor know of our decision. Now he REALLY thought we were crazy!!! He told us he was getting some resistance from some of his colleagues and the hospital staff where I would be delivering. Once again, Mary, director of Pediatric and Bereavement Services at the hospice, intervened on our behalf.

(Donna, mom of Jonathan who
was born with Potter's Syndrome)

Authoritative Comments

Doctors can be casual in unsettling ways. If your doctor calls you by your first name, call her by her first name. It is demeaning to be called Beth if you must call your physician Dr. Green. If your doctor starts to make small talk about your family, make small talk about his family. Being personable goes two ways.

You may also hear any of several authoritative comments:

- ✤ *You have to decide quickly.* Ask: "Why? What if we wait?"
- ✤ *You need to trust your doctor.* Ask: "How many cases like this have you seen? May we speak to other parents who have had children like this? How many babies like this have you delivered? I am going to seek another opinion."

❧ *Do not research the condition. Too much information will be confusing.* Ask: "Do you think we are too stupid to understand what we may find out? How could more information be confusing when we are already terribly confused with very little information?"

❧ *You do not really understand what you are dealing with. You are in denial.* Ask: "Are you saying that, because I have hope and because I want to move forward with the pregnancy, that automatically means that I am in denial? Why do you find it hard to believe that we want to give birth to and nurture our child?"

My obstetrician/gynecologist had been treating me for non-ovulation and had often rebuked me when I would ask her to let me go off the pill just to see what would happen. It seemed her attitude was that I should have accepted my infertility and enjoyed my career and sexual freedom. The fact that I was pregnant seemed to annoy her. She estimated I was three months pregnant and took blood to screen for Down syndrome among other conditions. My doctor called to let me know that our baby was going to suffer from severe Down syndrome. She delivered the news in a tone that seemed to say, "I told you being fertile and having children was not as wonderful as you thought." She suggested Michael and I discuss what we "wanted to do." I told her that we would be having our baby. She insisted that we seek counseling in order to "cope." She also suggested I have an amniocentesis. I said that we would not need an amniocentesis. She certainly made me feel like I was making poor decisions. She treated me with a minimum degree of respect. I should have found a doctor who supported our decisions and who would help us celebrate our baby's birth.

(Lisa, mom of Brady who was born without Down syndrome)

❧ *Your baby is suffering.* Ask: "What evidence do you have that our baby is suffering or will suffer? What can be done to alleviate suffering?"

❧ *Completing the pregnancy is emotionally unsound as your grieving will be too intense.* Ask: "Is this your opinion or has this been proved by medical research? How can you know how we will grieve?"

❧ *The baby is going to die anyway so why not end it now and try again?* Ask: "Are you telling us that, if our four-year-old were diagnosed with terminal leukemia, we ought to end his or her life at the time of diagnosis? Would you give this advice if your mother received a diagnosis of terminal cancer?"

❧ *Your child will never_____ (fill in the blank — go to Harvard, hold a job, have a family, walk, speak, etc.).* Ask: "Are you measuring the value of life by what a person can potentially achieve? Are you therefore implying that all people who cannot _____(fill in the blank as the doctor did) ought to be terminated? If your child acquired a disability as the result of a car accident and could never do _____ (fill in the blank as the doctor did), would you terminate him?"

My son Nick was born twelve years ago. I can recall the sounds and smells of the hospital, the look on the faces of the nurses, the dismal prediction of my son's life given to me by the pediatric neurosurgeon on call, my feelings of hysteria and confusion. His predictions of my son's quality of life could not have been more dismal if he would have walked up to me with a piece of black construction paper and told me, "This is your son's life. " He made sure I knew how dependent he would be on others, how he could not possibly be able to walk or have any meaningful function of his body, I never, and I mean never, accepted that as fact. I listened carefully to everything I was told, I read every bit of literature about spina bifida I could get my hands on, but I settled within myself that "we would see." My son has undergone many painful surgeries and, while I would not choose this for my child, this is my son. His life by some standards may not be easy. I would be hard pressed to name someone that had an easy time in their lives, regardless of disability. In twelve years of being Nick's mom I've learned many wonderful lessons. What does my son feel like, having a disability? He's a happy young man. He doesn't spend his time feeling sorry for himself. I see him pushing himself beyond all limits that others have placed on him.

(Ashley, mom of Nick who
was born with spina bifida)

🙠 *Your child will be a burden on society.* Ask: "Are you saying that our child is not worth what it would cost to treat him or her?"

🙠 *Your baby may have to endure _____ (fill in the blank with "a lot of tests and procedures," "mental retardation," "physical disability," "people staring," etc.) so why make him or her suffer?* Ask: "Are you saying that there is no medication for these tests and procedures? Are you saying that the benefit of these procedures is negligible because they might cause suffering while they are being done? How do you weigh the value of a procedure against the outcome of improved health? Do you believe that it is better to be dead than to live with mental or physical disability?"

At my fourth month prenatal exam, the doctors said, "We see one hand and the left hand looks like it is missing some digits. It does look like she has a thumb, but we don't feel there is any bone in that thumb. This could be caused by amniotic band syndrome which is very common. Fibrous amniotic bands are floating in the uterine fluid, and, if these wrap around a limb or digit, they can restrict blood flow and cause damage." They brought a counselor back in. They did say, "You have options. You can terminate this pregnancy." My husband and I said, "Options? We are talking about a perfectly healthy baby except for a few fingers missing. There are no options here. We will be here to talk with her about it."

*(Annalee, mom of Brooke who was born
with nodules for fingers and a boneless thumb on her left hand)*

❧ *Your other children will be affected because your baby will never be a real participant in family life.* Ask: "How do you know what this child's influence on our other children will be? What proof do you have?"

My own children have grown in comparison and understanding from being exposed firsthand to Alex's needs [*Alex had leukemia*] so I do not fear that I am placing a burden on them by bringing Sidney to our family. I feel instead that I am giving them something precious that will help to set them apart in a good way and make them better parents, better friends, and better contributors to society. Giving my kids this valuable experience will teach them to handle adversity in their lives, care better for their own children, face death if need be and know they can survive, and to care for the elderly in their lives better than they could otherwise do. These are things you cannot teach by just telling them. They must experience the rewards of giving of themselves to someone who can give nothing back except love. This is why I want Sidney to live long enough to come home. Because I know that she can help our family be a better family.

*(Laura, mom of Sidney who
was born with a lethal form of dwarfism)*

❧ *You will experience a financial and emotional drain in caring for this child.* Ask: "Are you familiar with the financial and emotional status of our family? If not, what would cause you to say this?"

❧ *There is a high divorce rate among parents of children with disabilities.* Ask: "Are you aware that marriages fail at the same rate when pregnancies are terminated due to disability?"

More Information

You may *not* be told that:

❧ Your child with a fatal diagnosis could be born alive and live for a short time after birth.

- ❧ You can speak with other parents who have borne children with the same condition as your child.
- ❧ You can receive help from parent support groups.
- ❧ There are false positives for some of the prenatal tests.
- ❧ No one can tell with certainty the degree of disability.
- ❧ Many doctors have never seen or treated a child with your condition and do not know what to expect.
- ❧ No one can tell with certainty what your child will be able to do or how long he or she may live.

Menke's Disease is a fatal genetic disease, and we were told Nathan would not likely live to see his second birthday. He was very, very small all his life, and at his death (age fourteen) he weighed only sixteen pounds and was only thirty-six inches long. Despite all these problems, he was the happiest, most sunshiny child you could ever want to meet. His smile caught everyone by the heart, and held them there.

(Jennifer, mom of Nathan who
was born with Menke's Disease)

- ❧ There are many parents who have given birth, knowing in advance that their children had this same condition.
- ❧ Having a child with difficulties strengthens some marriages.

There is absolutely no question that our marriage got stronger. I would go through a period of having a really hard time and Jack would be the strong one and then we would flip-flop and it seemed like one of us was always holding the other up. Kelsey was our second child. Megan, our first, helped us stay focused and get out of the hospital and do fun things. We knew we had to have a life for Megan. We have some friends who have a child with disabilities. They ended up divorcing, but I think a big part of it was the mother's attitude. Suddenly the other children and her husband were not getting attention because she was going to travel the world to make her son all better.

(Chylene, mom of Kelsey who
was born with CMTC Syndrome)

Medical Libraries and Online Information

You will want to obtain up-to-date information on your child's condition. Your physician may not be able to supply this.

I also telephoned the midwife, and like my uncle, she urged me to continue living normally and to give this baby everything I would give to a healthy child. She gave me a website address on anencephaly:

I could see for the first time pictures of newborns with anencephaly
and the testimonies of the affected parents. This helped me during
the following days, knowing that I was not alone. People have lived
through the same experience, and it is not completely crazy to keep
the baby. If the world cannot understand our decision, God does.

(Monika, mom of Anouk who
was born with anencephaly)

Much information is online and in medical libraries. Keep searching until
you find what you need. Share the information with your medical team.

I found this website to be very helpful: www.bladderexstrophy.com.
Also the book, *Living with Bladder Exstrophy*, that I ordered through
the bladder exstrophy website. I found the chat via this website the
most helpful. It connected me with others living through a similar
experience. I also frequented our local medical library where there
was an expert librarian who pulled information from websites and
bookmarked medical journals for me to read. Medical libraries can
be a big help. Usually the person working there really wants to
guide you to the best resources.

(Jennifer, mom of Mikey who
was born with cloacal exstrophy)

There is a technique to finding information via the internet.

When faced with a poor diagnosis, you want to know all you can
about it, and you want to know how to find hope. This is a combination of medical and technical info. I start with a Google search,
because it generally turns up the best medical searches.

To get started, use the common term. For instance,"dwarfism."
This will return hits of pages which are geared toward giving basic
information. This is also how you find the medical term for a condition or symptom.

If you really want to dig deep, then use the medical term as the
search term. For dwarfism, that would be "skeletal dysplasia." This
returns hits aimed more at the medical community. It also means you
may be buried in technical terms. You can do a search on Google
for the term you do not understand (time-consuming), or if you can
find a page that is in eMedicine.com, you can highlight a word and
it pops up a dictionary window with a definition in it. Best though,
is to just buy a medical dictionary. They are cheap. Bookmark the
pages that you think are worth looking at again.

A negative prenatal diagnosis may only be a collection of features.
We were told our daughter had short limbs, a constricted rib cage,
ventriculomegaly, potential heart abnormalities, and that I had poly-

hydramnios [*too much amniotic fluid*]. These features are typical of several types of short-limbed dwarfism, but most are in the "lethal" or "semi-lethal" neonatal types. Because we knew that the condition was a type of skeletal dysplasia, we were able to search on that. But often you have to start with the feature, and learn what conditions might contain that feature.

Even when you know the condition, it is wise to research the features separately. This helps you understand what each one means, and what treatment might be available. It also helps you to understand what else your child might have if the condition was misdiagnosed. Other diagnoses with similar features are called "differential diagnoses." On professional medical pages you will often find differential diagnoses listed, and you can research those also to understand what other conditions are similar. Treatments are offered for some similar conditions.

When using a search engine, to get varied information you really have to go five to ten pages deep. You also need to change your search terms in as many ways as you can think of — we researched "skeletal dysplasia," "curved femur," "bowed femur," "lung hypoplasia," "thanatophoric survival," as well as other combinations. I wanted to find not just the standard rhetoric, but the few pages that said something just a little different. It is only as you research more deeply that you find examples of the few exceptions, the ones that lived a little longer, the ones that were misdiagnosed, or the times when the condition was not as severe as first thought, or new treatments for less common conditions.

Personal pages provide another source of hopeful information. Those are usually buried pretty deep on the search engine pages. These pages, and sites which contain personal stories, are so very encouraging because they give day-to-day examples of living with both the diagnosis and the child, and they contain a range of outcomes. Reading them can help you to face the range of possibilities and to know that if that family could survive it, then you can too, even if you do not want to have to.

Researching can be VERY discouraging. Most medical information available on negative prenatal diagnoses focuses to a high degree on termination. A lot of the case studies are on aborted fetuses. These studies place much focus on the poor chances, and very little on the exceptions or the times when it turns out well. Ninety-nine percent of what you find will depress you. But if you can persevere and focus on the little bits you find that are good, the 1 percent that is hopeful may be the difference between you seeing your child as a lost cause and seeing that there is a chance for her to accomplish something exceptional. In fact, the medical community does not give much attention to the kids who make it. They seem to gloss over that. They say no child with thanatophoric dysplasia ever lived without a respirator, but I found two who did. They say that no child with Trisomy 13 has ever lived past the age of six months. I found a child with it who was two years old.

Even though some days were so discouraging as I found only the same negative information, I am glad I was able to search the net for information, because it provided the few grains of hope that I needed to believe my baby had a chance, no matter how small. And it prepared me to deal with her issues if she could in fact make it. I knew what support services she was likely to need, and I knew that, even though I did not want to have to learn some of what I needed to learn to care for her, that I could face it and do it.

(Laura, mom of Sidney who was
born with a lethal form of dwarfism)

Medical journals can supply much information, too. You may be able to research these at your local library and request copies through interlibrary loan. Many medical articles are online.

For just about every condition there are a number of medical journal articles. Just plug in the subject in the [*browser's*] search bar. Various articles will come up, and then you just have to dig through them for helpful information. I steer away from websites that are agenda-driven or merely devoted to general childhood illness, family medicine, etc. I want websites that give verifiable, reliable MEDICAL information, with sources and references that are well-documented. If I am looking for treatment information, I gather a good number of resources that appear to be reliable and verifiable, and then compare the conclusions and look to see if there is a consensus. I look at credentials and to see if the information is current. I look to see if the information presented seems biased or more of a personal point of view. There is a lot of quackery and medical misinformation presented as truth, and it's important to stay away from that. Use good judgment and care in picking resources and checking documentation.

(Jennifer, mom of Nathan who
was born with Menke's Disease)

The more you know, the better you can prepare yourself and your medical team for your child.

I worried about the challenges and sort of spent a season lamenting the loss of the dream of a normal child. I admit I didn't want Down syndrome, but I wanted my child, THAT child, and if he had it, then we'd all live with it. We read books about Down syndrome to try and better acquaint ourselves with what our life was more than likely about to become. Basically we just fastened our seatbelts and knew that, come what may, love would find a way. That's what love is.

(Ashli, mom of Emmil who was
born without Down syndrome)

Supportive Doctor

Search for a doctor who will support you and your baby. Having such a doctor makes all the difference in the world.

When we finally met our fetal cardiologist in person, we immediately sensed that she had a very positive approach. She spoke and behaved as though she wanted our baby to live. We believed that she would find a way to help us. She gave our baby a new diagnosis, HRHS (hypoplastic right heart syndrome). We were suddenly introduced to the world of chambers and valves and spontaneously produced pencil sketches of our baby's abnormal heart. The diagnosis was easier to take this time around because we had a plan to pursue. Soon after birth, our baby would have the first of three open-heart surgeries that would allow her heart to function with only one working ventricle.

(Monica, mom of Celine who was born with
hypoplastic right heart syndrome)

I spoke with the pediatrician. He treated me like a rational intelligent human being, and discussed potential issues and treatments. He had no problem with our wishes to give our daughter the tools

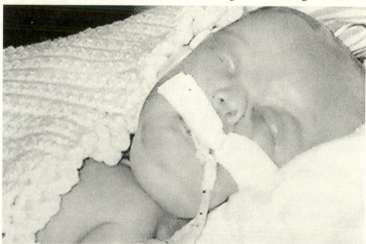

Tanner was diagnosed in utero with posterior urethral valves and was born when labor commenced naturally. His mother writes, "Although I knew my son was dying, I had never been happier in my whole life because he was the greatest gift I had ever received. I would do it all over again just for those wonderful thirty-six hours that we had with Tanner."

she needed to survive if she could, without forcing her to survive. He was the first doctor who was willing to look at more than just the diagnosis and actually assess her as an individual.

(Laura, mom of Sidney who was born
with a lethal form of dwarfism)

You may have to educate your doctor and hospital staff. Your doctor may never have delivered a child with your child's condition.

My obstetrician had never delivered a baby like this. My baby and I were going to be pioneers — and we needed to teach the professionals how to do this. My local hospital had never dealt with a case like this. My obstetrician told me to write up a birth plan, which, after much research, I did. Several weeks later, my obstetrician got the amnio results confirming full Trisomy 18. He told me that he knew we were dealing with "only one patient now." He also said that we would have a regular delivery instead of a C-section. (Before Grace was diagnosed, my previous children were C-sections and she was going to be one, too.) Also he said it wasn't important to monitor her. I left the office feeling uneasy. I called a "pro-life doctor." I told him I wanted to switch to him. He was friends with my OB, and told me that he would talk to my OB and to give him another chance. During the next visit I grabbed the doctor by the shoulders and said, "Look, if you don't see me and my baby as two patients, I can't work with you!" He said, "I know, I know, I talked with Dr. S. and he told me that you called him. I understand. All you want is to hold your baby for five minutes. You tell me what you want and I'll do it." From that point on, all the decisions revolved around maximizing the chance of having a live baby. My OB told me he will never be the same. Grace had a profound impact on the doctors that worked with us. My OB took my birth plan and distributed it to all of the nursery/OB staff and had meetings with them to plan the delivery. I met personally with the head nurse of labor and delivery as well as with the head nurse of the nursery, the neonatalogist, and the VP of the hospital. Much planning went into Grace's arrival. As the nurses told me, "Chris, there wasn't a protocol written to do this kind of thing. You wrote the protocol."

(Christine, mom of Grace Ann who
was born with Trisomy 18)

4

PARENTING OPTIONS

Be patient with everyone, but above all with yourself.[1]

Francis de Sales

Nathan

I admire my brother Nathan.

The reason is because he is handicapped and still is happy, and never complains.

He has Menke's Kinky Hair Disease.

It is a very rare disease, and it is a very hard word.

He is five years old right now.

Another reason I love him is because he almost died a few weeks ago!

He is patient and tries hard.

He is happy, cute, has a cute giggle, and he doesn't cry very much.

He's very gentle.

He is always sick but doesn't complain.

He can't do very much.

He can't talk or walk, but he really enjoys watching me dance and play.

He smiles a lot and he loves me a lot.

He likes people to sing to him.

Inside he is like everybody else.

He teaches me to be brave.

I love him and admire him very much.

Emilie Elisabeth Saks, age seven, sister of Nathan
who was born with Menke's Disease

If you are like most people, you like to feel in control of your life. Receiving a serious prenatal diagnosis can make you feel powerless.

Shortly after we received our news *[that our unborn child had Down syndrome]*, severe panic attacks began to interfere with my sleep at night. Soon, they would hit hard and strong during the day as well. These were due to my own personality type. I like to have

---

1. http://www.visitationmonastery.org/stlouis/Counsels.htm.

things under control and, if they are not under control, I want to fix it. And this was something I couldn't control.

(Nina, mom of Tess who
was born with Down syndrome)

Even though you like to be in control, sometimes that is impossible. Although you know how important good planning is, probably you have lived through unexpected experiences that forced you to make unanticipated decisions. Expectations did not materialize while unforeseen consequences did. Right now, many questions about your baby cannot be answered with certainty. Take one day, even one moment, at a time. Try to enjoy your baby now. You will live through the future when it arrives.

Grace was the most helpless creation — she brought out the goodness of people. Grace provided an opportunity for many people to love unconditionally. People couldn't do enough for our family. The hospital bent over backwards for us. My friends and family continue to support and love us. Grace did more in two months than some people do in a lifetime. She was pure love, and she experienced pure love. I thank God He blessed us with her. She was worth it all.

(Christine, mom of Grace Ann
who was born with Trisomy 18)

The Immediate Choices

Parents who receive a serious prenatal diagnosis face the immediate choices of how to view the situation. Some of these choices are:

- ❧ To fear the future or to go forward in confidence.
- ❧ To grieve for your imagined child or to love your actual child.
- ❧ To be overwhelmed by questions or to research answers.
- ❧ To give up in despair or to fight discouragement.

Some days I was so discouraged. After a day of depressing reading, I wondered what difference it would make anyway. But each time I considered giving up and not trying to help her live, I felt so dark and awful that I knew it was not what I needed to do. I believe this baby was sent to me because I WOULD fight. I think she came to our family because we could accept her completely, and love her regardless of her limitations or how short her time.

(Laura, mom of Sidney who
was born with a lethal form of dwarfism)

- ❧ To see this diagnosis as the end of your world or to see it as the beginning of a new world.
- ❧ To consider this pregnancy a disaster or an opportunity.

✎ To view your child as a genetic blunder or as a serendipitous gift.

✎ To focus on the pain in each day or to seize the joy.

> First I didn't believe that our child had a fatal condition. I was always optimistic that there had been a big mistake, but I was not getting any bigger and he was not moving much. Then I went through a brief period of thinking, "What's the point? He's going to die anyway." Then I realized that if this baby wasn't going to live, this was my only chance to be his mom. I didn't know how much longer we had. I can look back and say I did everything to protect and nurture him the only way I could.
>
> *(Sandy, mom of Casey who was born with Trisomy 18)*

✎ To pinpoint the suffering or to transform the suffering into triumph.

✎ To close in on yourself or to reach out to others who can help.

✎ To deny your feelings or to acknowledge them.

✎ To cave in to negativity or to reject it.

> We had so little time left to enjoy her presence, but in that time, she taught us many silent lessons on the nature of love. During those last months that I carried Clare, my life was interwoven with intense joys and sorrows. Our Lord was so close that I expected to meet him around every corner, and in fact I did, in the eyes and the words and the actions of the faithful people he placed in my path.
>
> *(Elizabeth, mom of Clare Catherine who was born with anencephaly)*

✎ To cling to your world or to enter your child's world.

✎ To do what others think best or to let your child show you what is best for him.

✎ To isolate your child or to fully integrate her into society.

✎ To see life with your child as a dead end or as an extraordinary opportunity.

> The decision on whether to carry or terminate was a hell no parent should have to go through. I have never believed in abortion, but my first thought was, "How can I get out of this?" I did think about terminating. Who really doesn't? I think I was in shock and am now glad I took time to think this decision through. I asked God for a sign. He literally gave me one. I drove past a church that always has a sign with a daily message. This day it said, "Regret looks back. Faith looks up." I knew then that I had been fooling myself if I thought I could terminate. Only God can decide when a life ends. I felt like I would be killing one of my children. I would not do that to my other

kids. I did not want to look back in regret. My husband felt the same way. My pregnancy was hard both emotionally and physically, but each kick from this little life showed me it was worth it. This was the only time I was going to have with this child so I was going to enjoy it as much as possible. I also decided that I could be angry or that I could continually feel sorry for myself, but what would it change? If I accepted God's plan, I would honor my child more than if I were an angry mess. Don't get me wrong — there were days I had a hard time even getting out of bed, but when I didn't have the strength to go on, I prayed and God sent me His strength.

(Sue, mom of Lucas Adam who
was born with anencephaly)

The first choices will drain your energy and poison your spirit. The second ones will energize you. You may not be ready to embrace fully the second choices right now, but aim toward them anyway.

I am fully aware of the "cost" of raising such a child, in terms of illness, education, and family support. We have already frequented cardiology, gastroenterology, and audiology departments of local hospitals. There have already been plenty of sleepless nights as we struggle to keep him gaining weight; and this is just the first three months. But I also know that such children and adults draw out of us optimism, creativity, and patience in a way no "normal" child can. Such true "children" offer a reminder that the value of our life is not measured by what we achieve but by how much we love. The future will bring many more challenges, but we are confident that, as we accept the gift of his life, we will see how our lives are enriched. Benjamin is a person, unique, whole, to be loved, who will bring to us far more than we can ever give him.

(Eldad, dad of Benjamin who
was born with Down syndrome)

Support One Another

It is critical that those closest to the baby support one another.

At fifteen weeks gestation, we found out that one of our twin babies had died. At nineteen weeks gestation, our baby daughter Lucy was diagnosed with an omphalocele, where the intestines develop outside the body. We were advised to abort. We were told that our baby would either be a real "inconvenience," or worse, she would die minutes after birth. We decided that we would take her whatever way she came, and would not regret it. This is a poem I wrote to her after she was born.

Dear Lucy,

As I sit at your bedside today, you, my beautiful five day old daughter, I think of your father.

I THINK OF YOUR FATHER, Lucy, the man who held my hand tightly as we saw your tiny, twinkling, blinking heart on the ultrasound screen next to the very small, still body of your twin.

I THINK OF YOUR FATHER, Lucy, the man who let me sob on his shoulder after the doctor told us you had a fatal birth defect. I looked outside her office on that gray day, my tears mixing with your father's as our dreams for you fell apart.

I THINK OF YOUR FATHER, Lucy, the man who refused to end the life of a child he may hold for only a few minutes after birth, as she took her last breaths.

I THINK OF YOUR FATHER, Lucy, the man who cried tears of joy as you entered this world, sputtering and coughing, the heavens opening up and shining on the three of us as you were bundled up and carted away for surgery.

I THINK OF YOUR FATHER, Lucy, the man who called me with a quavering voice, telling me you had made it through perfectly. We cried together.

I THINK OF YOUR FATHER, Lucy, a man who knows what is right and does it, who stands up against the evils in this world, who leans on his faith in God instead of the world's knowledge to give him what he needs to be the rock for his little family. So, my little Lucy, when you don't know what to do, when the world is telling you one thing and your convictions tell you another, just do what I do. Think of your father.

(Rachel, mom of Lucy who was born with an omphalocele which was surgically corrected)

Often mothers and fathers have different reactions to the pregnancy.

My husband felt more out of control. It is hard for men to see their wives suffering — they want to fix it but they can't. My husband could be detached from the pregnancy, even forget it for a few hours, but I carried our dying son around twenty-four hours a day. It was hard for my husband to watch me go through that. Men get over the pregnancy differently, too. It's not as intense for them. The hormones that get you ready physically and emotionally for the baby are still there even if the baby dies. The day of Casey's funeral my milk came in. All those chemicals get you ready for the job to do and you don't have it to do. It's not the same for the husband. The baby does not really seem real to him until he or she is born.

(Sandy, mom of Casey who was born with Trisomy 18)

Talk to your spouse about what you are feeling.

> Sidney's problems were so big, and so scary, my husband did not want to have to think about them. When I talked to him about her, he sort of tuned out and went away! One morning I told him that I felt like I had eight kids, and he had seven. I pointed out that he never spoke of her, had never said her name, and let him know how lonely and isolated I felt. At the time I was battling doctors to get them to acknowledge that she had value, and I needed his support, and told him so. He did try after that. He began making an effort, and it got easier for him to face things as he took the time to make jokes about my stomach, or to pat it as I went past. I have even heard him refer to her by name.
>
> *(Laura, mom of Sidney who*
> *was born with a lethal form of dwarfism)*

One way to foster communication is by writing letters to one another. Each parent should tell the other the troubling things the other does or does not do. Set a date to be alone for several hours. On the day of the date, each buy a rose. Exchange roses and letters. Talk about the content of the letters and how to solve the problems shared.[2]

Continue the communication. Have a date with one another weekly. No exceptions. Continue this practice no matter what parenting option you choose and whether or not your baby lives.

Parenting Options

Your baby may not be expected to live long. Your main job will be to parent your child for as long as life remains. Your other children may want to share their ideas about their baby brother or sister.

> The doctors and nurses tried to convince us to put Joey into a hospice — to not take him home but to visit him there. My husband thought maybe that was best for the other kids although I wanted to take Joey home. Our fifteen-year-old daughter Nora said, "You have to take him home. He's our brother and he needs us. We need to know him." So my husband said, "Let's go get him."
>
> *(Erin, mom of Joey who*
> *was born with Trisomy 18)*

However, your baby may not have an immediately fatal condition. Your child may live for months, years, or a lifetime. Later chapters will discuss long-term parenting. However, not everyone feels emotionally, physically, or spiritually qualified to parent a child with disabilities. Before your baby is born, you may want to explore alternate parenting choices:

---

2.   Simons, 28.

৯ Respite Care — Respite care means having others care for your
   child part of the day, either in your house or elsewhere. Check with
   community agencies regarding respite care.

৯ In-Home Nursing Care — Check with governmental agencies to
   determine if your child qualifies for government-funded nursing
   care in your home.

৯ Babysitting — A neighbor, friend, or family member may be able to
   care for your child part of the day.

৯ Foster Care — Use temporary foster care if you are trying to decide
   whether or to choose adoption or out-of-the-home care. Your government office can refer you to foster care services.

Adoption

Parents have many reactions to adoption:

৯ *I could never give up my child.* You are not giving up your child.
   You are giving your child the opportunity to have parents who feel
   qualified to raise him.

৯ *We conceived our child so it is our job to parent.* Maybe and maybe
   not. Maybe you conceived this child so that someone else could
   parent.

৯ *Why would God have given us this baby if not to raise?* We learn
   many things from our pregnancies and from all our experiences.
   There may be other reasons that God gave you this child.

৯ *I would always wonder what happened to our child.* You can make
   an open adoption plan, keep in touch with the adoptive family, and
   know.

We have a little adopted daughter, Hope, who has Down syndrome
just like our birth daughter, Tess. Her birth mom's first reaction was,
"I have to have an abortion," but she didn't really want to. Someone
told her, "You don't have to have an abortion. Let me point you in
the direction of adoption." Adoption is a greater option than we ever
thought. We include Hope's birth parents in our lives. We were in
contact the first year and we asked if her birth parents wanted to
participate in Hope's first birthday. We went to their home town, and
they invited friends and family, all who had given the birth mom a
baby shower with gifts for the adoptive family. They were able to
bring closure to their own grief. We are making plans for her second
birthday and will have those folks attend also. The birth mother is
now married. She and I had built a rapport with one another because

Lucy was diagnosed in utero with an omphalocele, which was surgically corrected.

no other two human beings are linked like we are because of this baby. The Lord has put it on our hearts to be as open as we are.

(Nina, mom of Tess and Hope
who were both born with Down syndrome)

❧ *What would others say if we made an adoption plan?* What does it matter? No matter what you choose, someone is going to disagree.

❧ *What would I say to others who ask about our baby?* How about, "Our baby is happy with his (her) adoptive family and we are delighted he (she) is there, too."

❧ *How could I answer the question, "How could you do such a thing?"* How about, "Every parent does what is best for their child. This was best for ours."

❧ *How would I handle the guilt that someone else is willing to parent my child but I am not?* By not taking on any guilt. Everyone has dif-

ferent abilities and talents. You are to be commended for admitting
that you are not emotionally and/or physically capable of caring for
your baby. Adoption puts the baby first. You deserve praise.

∽ *What will I say to our other children?* How about the truth? In
terms your other children can understand, explain why you made an
adoption plan for their brother or sister. Assure them that this plan
applied to this baby because it was best for him or her. Their staying
with mom and dad is best for them.

∽ *What will I say if someone asks how many children we have?* Either
tell them that information is not their concern, or else say, "____
with us and ____ being parented by others. Thanks for asking. How
about you?"

∽ *How will I deal with what others may think of us?* Try not to second-
guess other people. For every person who thinks negatively of you,
more will think positively. No one can please everyone. When you
make a decision that is right for you and your child, you have nothing to justify and every reason to be proud.

Many families wish to adopt children with disabilities. Agencies that
specialize in these adoptions can put you in touch with adoptive parents.
Talk to some of these families. You may understand better how they dif-
fer from yourself in parenting style. You can imagine how such parents
will be a good choice for your child.

> [*In striving to adopt a child with difficulties,*] we visited three
> orphanages in three different [*European*] towns to take pictures and
> get information about other children with disabilities and medical
> problems for our adoption agency. We visited a little girl who also
> has spina bifida. She was doing great and was up walking and talking.
> [*The adoption agency*] was able, later, to find a family for her and she
> is now in Oklahoma! We also visited the very large and well funded
> orphanage for young children. Sandy [*from the adoption agency*] had
> sent me a picture of a little girl there (eighteen months at the time)
> who didn't look very good. Her eyes gazed off in the picture and her
> head was huge and funny-shaped. We had just a funny feeling about
> her. She also was diagnosed with spina bifida. Before getting to see
> her, we spent time with other children, one with Down syndrome,
> one who is blind and a few others — all are now in the U.S.!
>
> *(Katie, mom of Karlee Rose, Benal, and Nikki*
> *who were all born with spina bifida)*

Consult local agencies and private lawyers that handle adoption. Decide
whether private adoption with an attorney, or adoption via a certified
adoption agency will work better for you. Adoption agencies provide

counseling for birth and adoptive parents while lawyers generally do not, but a lawyer may be more willing to design a unique, tailor-made adoption plan that will work for you. According to Dr. Byron C. Calhoun, NATHHAN/CHASK (one agency that works for the adoption of hard to place infants and children) has "over three hundred families in the United States who will adopt a child no matter what the problem or life expectancy."[3]

> Jonathan was followed a year later by our daughter Madeleine. Then by Jesse, Daniel, and Justin, three baby boys with Down syndrome we adopted. When people express surprise that with our large family we would take on more with special needs, I tell them, "When we found out what a treasure we had in Jonny, we decided we wanted more."
>
> *(Barbara, mom of Jonathan, Jesse, Daniel, and Justin, who were all born with Down syndrome)*

Sometimes someone you know will volunteer to parent or adopt your child. If you would never consider this, gently let the person know, being sure to offer your thanks. If you would consider it, work with the potential adoptive parent and an adoption agency that will provide legal guidelines and counseling.

If you do consider adoption for your child, think through the following questions before your baby is born:

- Do you want to hold and get to know your baby?
- Do you want to breastfeed?
- Do you want a voice in selecting the adoptive parents?
- How much contact do you want with the adoptive parents after the adoption is finalized?
- Do you want to take the baby home from the hospital?
- If you do not take the baby home, where will he or she go until being adopted?
- What will temporary foster care be like for your child?
- What can be done to have your baby go from the hospital directly to the adoptive family?

Out-of-the-Home Care

At one time, institutional care was the norm for children born with certain conditions. Today some parents choose long-term foster care or nursing facility care for their children. Many nursing facilities are operated by private groups. Investigate these options carefully. Visit

---

3. Letter from Dr. Byron Calhoun to Mrs. Kathleen M. Morgan, 15 March 2005.

places that you are considering. Ask about the care your child will receive. Learn how you can be part of the team that cares for your child. If you are not comfortable, honor your feelings. Your choice should give you peace.

If you choose out-of-the-home care, you may be asked many of the same questions put to parents who choose adoption. Refer to the previous section for some ways to answer these.

Gaining Time to Make a Parenting Choice

You may wish to have someone else temporarily parent your child as a legal guardian while you finalize a parenting plan. A lawyer can advise.

Charity Yorgason's birth family placed Charity in foster care while they explored parenting her, choosing an institution, or making an adoption plan. In her first three weeks after birth, Charity, who was born with severe brain loss, alternately spent time with her birth family and her foster family as her birth parents wrestled with their parenting choice. Finally they selected adoption.[4]

Letters

Be at peace with your parenting decision. If you keep changing your mind, wait. Temporary foster care, or guardianship, or parenting your child yourself while you decide, can buy you time. Only when you feel comfortable with a choice for two to three months should you act on it.

No matter what you decide, someone is going to disagree. Accept that this will happen and ignore it. Your decision will be right for you. Be at peace about it.

If you select an alternate parenting option, writing a letter to family, friends, and coworkers can help explain your choice and give others an idea of how to respond. The adoption agency or institution can assist you in composing such a letter.

A sample letter might read:

Dear _____,

We cherish your love and support. Therefore we would like to share with you our parenting plan for little (*baby's name*) who was recently born with (*name of disability*). After much discussion, counseling, and honest soul-searching, we have realized that we did the best we could in bringing (*baby's name*) to birth. Now we want to do the best

---

4. Blaine M. Yorgason, *One Tattered Angel* (Draper, Utah: Gentle Breeze Publications, 1995), 47–48.

for him (her) for the rest of his (her) life. Realizing our own limits, we have lovingly chosen (*an adoptive family, name of institution, or whatever plan was chosen*) to parent (*baby's name*). We are delighted that he (she) will have the care that we would not be able to provide.

You may wonder if you ought to mention our baby around us. Yes, of course! We love (*baby's name*) and he (she) will always be ours. Please wish us well and (*baby's name*), too.

We appreciate your accepting our choice and respecting our privacy regarding the details.

Thanks for understanding.

Sincerely,

————————————

Grief

You may experience some grief when you choose an alternate parenting plan. The grief comes from several sources:

- You will miss your child.
- You may feel guilty for not doing the parenting yourself.
- You may grieve the child you wanted to raise.
- You may grieve for a changed perception of yourself as parent.

Talk over your feelings with someone you can trust.

Do not allow Mother's Day and Father's Day to be difficult. You made the best choice for your child. Celebrate these days in some way. Other holidays may also be painful. Send your child a gift on those days or, if you made a closed adoption plan, send a gift in your child's memory to a shelter or children's hospital.

5

Sharing the News

It is only possible to live happily ever after on a day-to-day basis.

Margaret Bonnano[1]

Today my little baby sister Gianna was born. She was a month early and suffered from trisomonial disorders. I went to the hospital today and saw her ... she was alive and breathing and struggling to hold on to that gift most precious to each and every one of us — the gift of life. Her little chest moved up and down and her little face had the expression that she was fighting as hard as she could in a noble battle.

She died today. My little sister left this world to move on to a better one. An innocent, fragile lovable human being; her struggles are over and she rests now in happiness and peace with God in Heaven.

How often do we take our lives for granted? We get so wrapped up in our own disappointments and failures, but we fail to realize that we have the greatest thing going for us. We are alive and can make anything out of the life before us. Each breath we take is a gift — life is short and while we have it we should do something good with it. My little sister had but a few hours, but she lived it out to the fullest.

(Patrick Nagurny, age eighteen, brother of Gianna who was born with Trisomy 13 and holoprosencephaly)

You may not have told others about your baby's difficulties. You may wonder who to tell and how to do it. Begin with those closest to you — your other children.

Telling Your Children

The first child to tell is the one in your womb. Your unborn child may not understand your words, but he will sense your emotions. Talking to your baby also helps you to work through your feelings.

We learned much about anencephaly, but we still feared for both of our unborn children. We experienced sadness, grief, helplessness, but also happiness and hope. I tried to be honest with myself and with my unborn daughters. I spoke to them and tried to prepare myself and my daughters for what was going to happen. I told Anna I was very happy

---

1. http://www.quoteworld.org/quotes/1676.

with her and very sad she could not stay with us. I told my daughters to enjoy each other's company as long as they were together, because they had to say goodbye after birth, or maybe before birth. I told Tess to be strong and brave and that it would be difficult for her, too. I tried to teach my unborn children the colors, sounds and music through my own senses, while Anna was still alive. I needed to do this, because I was certain Anna would never enter the world she was supposed to be born in.

(Tineke, mom of Tess and Anna,
who was born with anencephaly)

It is important to tell your other children the news about their sibling before they hear it from others who may present it in ways you dislike. Explain your baby's problems as best you can. Explain how these will affect the family. You do not need to tell every detail to your other children, but all you tell them should be true.

We decided to help Nathan and Sarah get to know their unborn sister and be ready for what would happen. We encouraged them to lean over mommy's tummy and say, "Hello, Abigail!" and "Wake up, Abigail!" At first, it was a very forced, false cheerfulness that we had with the kids. It was so painful to talk to her ourselves and to have them do it. But, over time, it became natural, and we started thinking of her as baby Abigail who we loved, not as baby Abigail who has Trisomy 18. The kids started hugging her and telling her "goodbye" when I left for work, and soon it just made me joyful and happy to see their love and to think of her, not painful like before. We told Nathan that Abigail was sick and might not live, and so at first whenever we talked about Abigail, he would ask, "But what about 'might not live'?" One day, he asked, "If she dies, will we have another baby in a few months?" He also asked, "How long will she live?" And one time he said, "Maybe she'll be well for one day." Sometimes it made me cry to answer his innocent questions and to think that he had to be asking those questions at his age. But he handled it very well, knowing that Abigail would be going to heaven to be with Jesus and that someday "he'd be old enough to go be with Jesus, too."

(Mindy, mom of Abigail who
was born with Trisomy 18)

Older children who know something about abortion may wonder why you are continuing the pregnancy. Appendix F contains a parable called "Melody Fruit" which can initiate discussion.

Oh God, what do we do? There is not just me and the baby to consider but our other kids, too. How can I ask them to watch me for the next five months getting bigger and knowing that this baby was going to die? That is not fair to them and how could they cope? Could they cope with either choice? How could I "terminate" this baby and tell them? They would never understand. If I lied to them and just told them the baby died, how can I lie to them? My head was spinning. We had to tell the kids. It was only fair. We told them that the baby was sick and was going to die. We didn't know when and there was nothing that anyone could do. We did not tell them what was wrong with the baby as I felt that they may not be able to handle that right now. Abby immediately became upset and started crying. Joe avoided everything by asking the little boys if they wanted to play. Jake and Pete didn't understand what was going on. I knew they would need a lot of support, whatever happened. I tried to find out as much as I could about anencephaly and to find other people who had been through this, but I was unable to because of my inexperience with the internet. The genetic counselor was not much help. I wanted pictures to get myself and family ready. I could only find one pencil drawing, which was helpful to show the kids but didn't meet my needs. Jake looked at the picture and said that he knew why the baby was going to die, because it didn't have a brain and you had to have a brain to live. He also struggled with why we would want to name this baby because if you don't have a brain you wouldn't know anyway. I explained that everyone needed a brain and when our baby got to heaven he/she would get one from God and so really would need a name. This worked for him! I would hear Joe crying to himself at night. He was very worried about something happening to me and needed reassurance. His grades began to slip and he became angry. We got very concerned when he lost all competitive drive with his sports and didn't seem to care anymore. We took him to a counselor and we talked. That finally helped. Pete accepted what was going on and one day climbed up on me and speaking to my stomach said, "Hello, little baby that is going to grow up in heaven." How beautiful! Abby also talked about her feelings to her friends and teachers and to us and she grieved normally.

(Sue, mom of Lucas Adam
who was born with anencephaly)

Relatives

Not all grandparents, aunts, uncles, and other relatives can initially accept a child with differences. Unsupportive relatives can create a great deal of stress. You, as parents, may have to assert your right to see things differently than your parents or other relatives do. You are mature enough to make your own decisions and this is your baby, not theirs.

After I told one relative about the baby's condition, I could not believe the response. "Well, you are over forty!" As if Gianna's condition was a result of a risk I had taken! And then, "It would be best to have this baby out of your body as soon as possible." I am at risk for preterm labor and normally am required to drastically limit my activities. I was shocked that this relative would suggest that I encourage labor. This was the only time I had with my child! But then I realized that this relative was concerned about me and did not want me to suffer.

(Doreen, mom of Gianna who was born
with Trisomy 13 and holoprosencephaly)

Educate your relatives and try to be patient with them as they come to accept this new family member. Be honest and truthful. You have nothing shameful to hide. By telling the truth, you will not have to admit to untruths later. You will also discover those who support you. If you feel that someone cannot respond charitably and calmly to certain details, do not share them. If asked, change the subject or simply say, "To us, that is a private matter."

Some comments border on accusation. You may hear:

- How can you bring that poor child to birth?
- Children should not be brought into this world to suffer.
- How can you justify the cost?
- What is this going to do to your family (marriage, other children, spouse)?
- You cannot handle things now. How are you going to handle this?
- What are you doing to yourself?
- Have you talked to the right people about this?
- I know what we would do if we were in this situation.
- I have seen babies with this condition and they are not pretty.

Resist arguing. People who comment like this do not want dialog. Take control by responding, "Thank you for your concern." If you are a religious person, you might add, "We are letting God be in charge." Then change the subject. The unsupportive person will soon get the hint that you are not going to justify or debate your decision.

Handling Comments

Dealing with people who are unaware of your baby's condition is sometimes easier than dealing with those who do know. If you do not want to divulge details, briefly reply to strangers' comments:

ๆ *"How are you feeling?" "Fine."*

ๆ *"When is the baby due?"* Tell them your due date.

ๆ *"Is it a boy or a girl?"* If you know, tell them.

ๆ *"I bet you are excited." "We sure are."*

People want to make things better. They may say things like "God gives special kids to special families" or "an angel touched your child" or "God wants to bring blessings to you and so he gave you this child." Some people say, "It could have been worse," or, "Well, at least you never have to worry about him or her _____(fill in the blank with something negative that your child probably will never be able to do)," or, "These children are always _____ (fill in the blank with a positive adjective like happy, sinless, good)." These well-meaning comments may hurt or irritate you. A simple response of, "Thanks. I appreciate your caring," acknowledges the speaker's good will.

> Emily acted like she could not hear, even with loud noises and screaming right by her head. When she had a hearing test done after the placement of her shunt, it came back that she had normal hearing but a delay in processing it in her brain. In the last three months, her hearing reaction has improved drastically. I have been told by friends, they don't know how I can handle it all with calmness; they would be going crazy. I look at Emily as a blessing, not a burden or hardship. You just have to take things one at a time.
>
> *(Sabra, mom of Emily who was born*
> *with enlarged ventricles in her brain)*

People may say the wrong thing.

> I knew that when I could bring my baby home, everything would be all right! I remember feeling upset that everyone was saying they were "SORRY"! Here I had just had a beautiful baby and all everyone could do was feel sad for us! I wanted to hear "CONGRATULATIONS" and all I got were condolences. A baby is a miracle!
>
> *(Susan, mom of Victoria Ann who*
> *was born with spina bifida)*

Work to forgive those who hurt with their words.

> Sometimes the nurses didn't know our baby's diagnosis and would make cheery inappropriate comments. Others just wanted to get away from me as if I had a disease they could catch. Accepting and trusting God was not quite enough. There was a choice in accepting with grace or accepting in anger and feeling sorry for myself. I chose to carry in God's peace and grace. That meant accepting not only the joys of my baby but also accepting and forgiving the stupid (for the lack

of a better term) comments of those who were well-meaning, those that didn't know our baby's diagnosis, and those who didn't agree with my carrying a child who would die. I actually had comments of "no brain, not human." I was congratulated by many strangers who didn't know how my heart wept at their words. Others seeing me with my four kids said, "Not another one! How are you going to manage another one?" Oh, please God, I wish!

(Sue, mom of Lucas Adam who
was born with anencephaly)

You may also be praised beyond measure.

I have been called a saint for carrying Luke. I have been told by many that they couldn't do what I did. I am not a saint, and you don't know what you can do until you are faced with it. While I carried Luke, God carried me. That is what made the difference. It was not my strength but God's and that strength is available to anyone who asks. The secret is in the asking.

(Sue, mom of Lucas Adam who
was born with anencephaly)

People First Language[2]

People First Language describes what a person "has," not what a person "is." Use this language when speaking about and to your child. This is the language used in this book.[3]

The terms "special needs," "handicapped," "disabled," and other terms that marginalize and put the condition first do not represent People First Language. These terms elicit pity and imply that individuals cannot function, much as a "disabled vehicle" cannot run. Children and adults with disabilities do not need pity. They need opportunities to lead ordinary lives and become all they can be (like everyone else). When we are thoughtful, we realize that all of us have some type of "disability." Perhaps you cannot sing, do trigonometry, or build a house. So what? You have other abilities, just like everyone else does. People First Language focuses on the person first, not the condition. Here are some examples of People First Language:

ɤ "My child has anencephaly" rather than "My child is anencephalic."

---

2. People First Language is an innovation of people with disabilities, created during the 1970s. See personal letter from Kathie Snow to author, 14 March 2007.

3. In telling their stories, some of the parents do not use People First Language. I have chosen to retain their own wording so as to suggest how they and others viewed their situations.

❧ "My child has Down syndrome" rather than "My child is Downs."

❧ "My child uses a wheel-chair" rather than "My child is disabled."

❧ "My child has a disability" rather than "My child is disabled."

A good way to begin seeing your child in a new light is by journaling all her achievements. Begin today and, in time, your child's mission will become apparent.

> God has created me to do Him some definite service. He has committed some work to me which He has not committed to another. I have my mission — I may never know it in this life, but I shall be told it in the next. Somehow I am necessary for His purposes.... I am a link in a chain, a bond of connexion between persons. He has not created me for naught. I shall do good, I shall do His work; I shall be an angel of peace, a preacher of truth in my own place.... Therefore, I will trust Him. Whatever, wherever I am; I can never be thrown away. If I am in sickness, my sickness may serve Him; in perplexity, my perplexity may serve Him; if I am in sorrow, my sorrow may serve Him. My sickness, or perplexity, or sorrow may be necessary causes of some great end, which is quite beyond us. He does nothing in vain; He may prolong my life, He may shorten it; He knows what He is about. He may take away my friends, He may throw me among strangers, He may make me feel desolate, make my spirits sink, hide my future from me — still, He knows what He is about.[4]

Support Systems

You need a support system! Through the internet, and sometimes through referral from others, you can find families who are awaiting birth or who have given birth to children whose condition is similar to that of your child. These families can be a tremendous support.

> It's a miracle that God let Maria and me find each other, that our babies have the same condition and the same due date. She knows exactly what I am feeling and I know exactly what she is feeling.
>
> *(Rosa, mom of Arianna who was born with anencephaly)*

Brad and I found out at sixteen weeks that our baby had spina bifida. We were devastated. The doctors and counselors gave us the worst-case scenario and pretty much scared us to death. They told us we had two weeks to make a decision; do we terminate the pregnancy or go on knowing that our baby would be born handicapped. So the

---

4. John Henry Cardinal Newman, *Taking on the Heart of Christ: Meditations and Devotions* (Denville, New Jersey: Dimension Books, 1976), 5.

work began. We read everything we could get our hands on; we visited a neurosurgeon and pediatrician. We contacted the Indiana Spina Bifida Association for information. We visited a family who has a daughter with spina bifida. We prayed and cried and talked and prayed. Finally, just a couple days short of our "deadline," we had dinner with a high school friend of Brad's who is paralyzed and uses a wheelchair. His was an industrial accident, but we wanted to get his perspective. We asked him how he feels about his life now. He's a wheelchair marathon champion. He's happy and healthy and productive. Seeing life from his view, we chose to bring Karlee Rose into the world.

(Katie, mom of Karlee Rose, Benal, and Nikki,
all of whom were born with spina bifida)

I went to the internet and found SOFT (Support for Families with Trisomy). I did manage to find some mothers who had live births. Most brought their kids home to bury them within a short time. They were women of all faiths and they were glad they had brought their kids home. They had a lot of technical support to do that. I even talked to one woman whose child lived to age thirteen. Everyone was negative other than those people whom I contacted through SOFT. I felt like I was on another planet. However, you do what you have to do. I tried not to let the negativity get me down.

(Emily, mom of Andrew who
was born with Trisomy 13)

Search, too, for adults who have grown up with the same condition as your child. Their insights can be particularly helpful.

I have Down syndrome. I am very smart and very bright. A Down syndrome baby[5] is very smart, they can walk, talk, and have many learning skills. As a Down syndrome adult I am able to learn many new things and develop many new skills. It seems as though people do not understand that. People must understand that the Down syndrome adult has much talent and they are able to learn and grow as anybody else can learn and grow. The Down syndrome person can learn so much in life. They have special teachers who help them. We are able to read newspapers, work on computers and like myself write poetry and stories. The Down syndrome person has much talent and uses that talent to learn and do many new things.

(Bob, an adult who was
born with Down syndrome)[6]

---

5. The author of this letter was unaware of People First Language.

6. Bob Lanouette, "Letter from an Adult with Special Needs." Appendix B in *Having Your Baby When Others Say No! Overcoming the fears about having your baby* (Garden City, New York: Avery, 1991).

Confide in your employer. You may find much support in the work environment.

> I work with a wonderful group of people who were there for me every single day. I could be myself with them and they accepted me and my baby unconditionally. My bosses were supportive beyond words. I am forever grateful for these wonderful caring people and owe them my sanity and my everlasting gratitude.
>
> *(Sue, mom of Lucas Adam who*
> *was born with anencephaly)*

Social workers, clergy, doctors, psychologists, and psychiatrists can be helpful. Agencies provide information and assistance. Research these via the internet or consult some of the agencies listed in Appendix B of this book. If you need financial services, ask doctors, state agencies, and social workers to guide you.

> When things seem so hopeless, don't give up. There is help out there to assist you in keeping your baby. Lean on others for support.
>
> *(Shellie, mom of Dylan who*
> *was born with hydrocephalus)*

Sharing the News in Writing

Send out an email or a form letter to family and friends to let them know your baby's condition. Try to anticipate and answer all their questions. Let them know your plans and how you wish them to respond to you. Some people will respond positively. Others may feel that you need to be alone or else are not sure what to say and will not respond.

> I had let the school and my kids' friends' parents know. The kids were going to need all the support they could get. I also am very active in the school and all the kids know me and would be struggling to understand. Everyone pitched in to help my kids. There were many group hugs. I had many kids come up to me with questions and comments. How wonderful kids are in their innocence! I remember one little girl who in a very serious voice said, "Mrs. Jorgenson, I am very sorry about that dead baby inside your tummy." Then she skipped off before I could answer. How much better than some adults that just plain avoided me!
>
> *(Sue, mom of Lucas Adam who*
> *was born with anencephaly)*

Once you understand the baby's condition better, you may want to send a letter or email with ways that your family and friends can help you prepare for the baby's birth. Often, people don't know what to do in a situation like this, and they appreciate knowing how they can help. You can ask people to help you by:

- Finding other informational resources on the baby's condition for you.

- Watching your other children (if any) so you can make phone calls or go to appointments.

- Making phone calls for you, or going to medical appointments with you.

- Helping out financially or organizing a fundraiser for you if you will be traveling or need to cover certain costs.

- House/pet sitting if you are going to travel.

- Cleaning your house.

- Making prepared dinners for you prior to, or after the baby's arrival.

- Organizing a blood drive — either for the general pool, or for a directed blood donation for your baby (Ask your physician about directed blood donations.)

- Adding you and the baby to prayer lists.

- Throwing a baby shower for you, if you would like. Some parents decide that they prefer to wait until the baby is home and then have a baby shower/welcome home party. Others want to proceed as normal and have a baby shower while pregnant. Make sure that you make your wishes known to family and friends, whatever you decide.

- Beginning a "Random Act of Kindness" campaign in the baby's name. Asking people to do a nice thing for someone else while waiting for the baby can help create special meaning and purpose to the baby's life before he or she even arrives. Ask family and friends to send you a note of their act of kindness, so you can keep a record of the positive impact your baby has had on the world.

By clearly communicating your needs and expectations to family members and friends, you can eliminate misunderstandings, and receive the support and help you need during this very difficult time.

(Debbie Hilton Kamm, Mother of Braedon who was born with hypoplastic left heart syndrome)[7]

---

7.   Debbie is creator of the HLHS Information website (www.HLHSinfo.org) and co-founder of California Heart Connection (www.caheartconnection.org), a nonprofit support network for those with heart defects. Revised April 26, 2005.

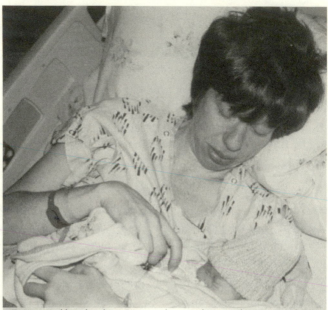

Doreen and her daughter Gianna who was diagnosed in utero with Trisomy 13 and holoprosencephaly. Gianna lived a short time after birth.

Bethany's depiction of her baby sister Gianna's entry into heav-
en. Gianna was born with Trisomy 13 and holoprosencephaly.

6

Birth and Death Plans

The fear of death keeps us from living, not from dying.

Paul C. Roud[1]

Forever Mother

My sweet baby Gianna,
When others do not know you or forget you
FOREVER I will remember you,
FOREVER I will love you,
FOREVER my heart will ache for you,
FOREVER I will hear the loud steady beats of your heart,
FOREVER I will feel your strong kicks inside of me.
My other children will grow and move on to the places that life
    takes them;
FOREVER you will reside within me.
FOREVER I will remember the moment you were born, the moment
    you began to die.
FOREVER I will recall your sweet scent, your light breath.
FOREVER I will long to hold you in my arms and
Trace my finger along your lips and ears.
FOREVER I will feel the softness of your hair, your skin.
You have transformed me
FOREVER.
FOREVER I will pray to you
Until we meet again in HEAVEN.
FOREVER I will thank God for giving me the greatest gift,
FOREVER I will know His LOVE, His JOY, His HOPE.
Sweet Baby Gianna,
I will love you FOREVER.

Doreen M. Nagurny, mom of Gianna
who was born with Trisomy 13 and holoprosencephaly

If you have received the news that your baby has a fatal condition, you are trying to adjust to your baby's birth and death. Your time with your baby is very limited. The time to love and nurture your baby is now. There may not be too much additional time.

---

1. http://www.artscraftsshowbusiness.com/thoughts.htm.

I knew as soon as she came out of my body the clock started to tick. Time was running out. I was prepared for a very short life for Grace. I even thought that maybe her time inside me was all I would get. I cherished every kick and move she made.

(Christine, mom of Grace Ann
who was born with Trisomy 18)

Where Is God?

As the parent of a dying child, you may question God. What is God doing? Here is a poem that may help:

Life's Weaving

My Life is but a weaving
Between my God and me;
I may not choose the colors,
He knows what they should be
For He can view the rainbow
Upon the upper side,
While I can see it only
On this, the under side.
Sometimes He weaves sorrow,
Which seems strange to me;
But I will trust His judgment,
And work on faithfully;
At last, when life is ended,
With Him I shall abide,
Then I may view the rainbow
Upon the upper side;
Then I shall know the reason
Why pain with joy entwined,
Was woven in the fabric
Of life that God designed.

author unknown[2]

Parents with faith generally resolve their questions about God, but it may take time.

First, God is in control. Medical technology revealed Abigail's genetic defect, but no medical technology could fix it. No expert could tell us how severe her problems would be. No doctor could tell us whether she would be stillborn. Only God knew when she would come into the world and how many days she would have. Although He didn't tell us how long it would be, He did speak to us. Through His word, He

---

2.   See http://nitewriter.net/lifesweaving.htm.

assured us that He would be with us. He would listen to our prayers. He cares. None of us knows the number of days He has given each of us. After a short time we could all be together again forever. And so in a time of grief and sorrow, we found comfort and peace and even joy.

(Steve, father of Abigail who
was born with Trisomy 18)

Perinatal Hospice

You may be fortunate enough to have access to a perinatal hospice. Perinatal hospice will support you from the time of your baby's diagnosis through the pregnancy, birth, and death of your child and into the post-partum period. Your local hospital or hospice will be able to tell you if a perinatal hospice is available.

I contacted Mary, the Assistant Vice President of Counseling Services and Director of the Perinatal and Pediatric Programs for Hospice Care Network. She had recently helped another mom who was pregnant with a baby with a fatal condition. Mary helped us create a birth plan so that our wishes would be honored. Because of Mary's help, Walter and I began to feel a sense of control. We gained the courage and strength to advocate on behalf of our unborn child. Mary acted as a liaison between my doctor and me and also communicated with personnel at the hospital where I would be delivering. She provided bereavement support to my children on a weekly basis. Mary had also put me in contact with the other mom whom she recently helped.

(Donna, mom of Jonathan who
was born with Potter's Syndrome)

We really didn't need a lot of nursing care, we were the nurses. We did have a volunteer come in once a week, so I could spend time alone with my two other girls. If anyone brings a baby like this home, hospice is the way to go. They were great.

(Christine, mom of Grace Ann
who was born with Trisomy 18)

If you do not have a perinatal hospice nearby, you can work with your physician and hospital staff to create a plan that works best for you.

Birth Plan

By creating a birth plan, you are able to control certain aspects of your delivery. Most medical personnel are grateful for birth plans. Decades ago, dead or dying babies were whisked away in the mistaken idea that keeping the parents from seeing them spared unnecessary anguish. Birth plans help the medical staff know how you want them to treat you and your child.

Your initial consideration will be: Do you want comfort care or aggressive management for your child? Discuss both options with your doctor, and be sure that both you and the doctor understand the terms in the same way.

> Two terms are bandied about: "aggressive management" (or "heroics"), and "comfort care." Parents need to discover what those terms mean to the medical personnel and the facility they choose. To one doctor, "comfort care" will consist of wrapping the child in a blanket and handing him to the parents. To another, comfort care includes feeding tubes, oxygen, and medicine to treat infections or other conditions. One doctor may consider "aggressive management" to be any help at all to a potentially terminal infant; another may consider it to be only life support and other extreme measures. We wanted a middle road. We wanted Sidney to have care, but not to be forced to live.
>
> *(Laura, mom of Sidney who*
> *was born with a lethal form of dwarfism)*

Once you determine a treatment option, you will want to focus on other details of the birth. Devise a plan that will work for you, your family, and your baby.

Do you want:

- To have a private room?
- To take photos?
- To videotape the birth and the baby?
- To have your children or others present at the birth?
- To have visitors after the baby is born?
- To breastfeed or express breast milk for your baby?
- To have a naming ceremony?
- To have a member of the clergy present?
- To bathe your baby?
- To have your baby with you all the time?
- To have your partner sleep in the room with you and the baby?
- To have footprints and handprints of your baby?
- To have molds of the baby's feet and hands?
- To keep mementos such as the baby's blanket, cap, lock of hair, clothes the baby wore?

Record your wishes in the birth plan.

Share the birth plan with your physician and, when he or she agrees to it, have the final birth plan signed and notarized. Ask your physician if you should share the plan with the hospital staff in advance or bring copies to the hospital when you are in labor. It is critical that everyone involved in the delivery know and follow your birth plan.

I made a birth plan. We wanted no heroics. We wanted our child to die naturally and without pain and to be respected as the human being he/she was. I met with the director of nursing so the hospital would honor my requests. It was no problem I was told. We wanted the kids to be as involved as they could be. We already had a girl's name picked out — Janet Ruth, after my grandmother and Doran's mother. Joe and Abby picked the boy's name. Joe liked Luke and Abby liked Adam so it became Lucas Adam.

(Sue, mom of Lucas Adam who
was born with anencephaly)

A lot of resources were pulled together to create the birth plan: internet, Fetal Treatment Center, palliative care specialists. We were blazing new territory at our hospital; usually this type of situation is transferred to a larger hospital that sees this more frequently. Some of the things we wanted were out of the ordinary and required us to make arrangements ahead of time. So we had to meet with the neonatologists and the pediatrician who would be handling Abigail's palliative care.

(Mindy, mom of Abigail who
was born with Trisomy 18)

Here is the birth plan which was used for Jonathan's birth:

Birthplan
Victoria Lynn or Jonathan Steven Dobkowski

Written by parents, Donna and Walter Dobkowski,
(Revised April 13, 2003)

We have known for months that our unborn baby has been diagnosed with bilateral renal agenesis, also known as Potter's Syndrome. We have made an informed decision to carry this baby to term and keep our baby as long as possible. It is our priority to have our baby born alive. Please honor our request to preserve the dignity of our baby's life. Please respect our following decisions:

❧ We would like staff to be informed and aware of the situation.

❧ Donna would like an epidural during labor. If complications arise for the baby during labor, in order to maximize the chances for a live birth, then we would like the option of having a C-section. We would want to properly medicate Donna so she does not have any pain during the procedure, but at the same time, we want to ensure that Donna is alert throughout it and that Walter is by her side. We want Donna to have the best physical outcome possible, but our primary goal is to ensure that our baby has every chance to meet us and that he/she is protected from unnecessary pain and suffering.

- We request that a liaison (nurse, social worker, chaplain) periodically give updates to waiting family members.

- If the baby is a girl, we would like her referred to as Victoria. If the baby is a boy, we would like him to be referred to as Jonathan.

- We would like the doctor to cut the cord.

- We would like for mechanical assistance (bagging only, no intubation) to be used only temporarily to try to initiate the baby's breathing, if necessary, immediately after birth. We do not want any extraordinary measures taken to maintain breathing or initiate a heartbeat. After this is performed and after wiping and wrapping the baby, we request that our baby be handed to Mom/Dad and that weighing the baby, labs and confirmation of the diagnosis be postponed until later.

- Our baby will be baptized as soon as possible after cutting the cord. This will be performed by Walter. We ask that the grandparents and our three children be present at this time if possible.

- We would like our baby to stay with us at all times.

- Our baby should be offered comfort care: feeding, bathing, swaddling and holding by his/her parents and family.

- We wish to be with our baby and hold our baby at the time of death.

- When our baby dies, we want some time to be together as a family alone.

- We would like to be alone, away from other newborns, before and after our baby's birth.

- We do not wish an autopsy to be performed.

- We would like to keep the following items as keepsakes:
  1. Bassinet card
  2. Hats
  3. Baby blanket
  4. Photos
  5. Hospital ID bracelet
  6. Handprints/footprints (we have plaster molds)
  7. Lock of hair
  8. Birth certificate
  9. Death certificate

To the staff of Labor/Delivery and Neonatal Units,

We have tried our best to prepare for this short time with our beloved baby. Thank you so much for helping us and supporting us through this celebration of our baby's short but precious and meaningful life.

Donna F. Dobkowski, mother
Walter A. Dobkowski, father[3]

Creating Memories

Memories begin now, before your baby is born. You may want to keep a journal. You might create a scrapbook of ultrasound or pregnant mom photos and/or other memorabilia. Or you may wish to have a family photo taken in which mom is clearly pregnant. Such a photo will actualize your baby's existence for the future. You may want to make your baby's blanket, cap, or outfit or select them from the store. If your baby has a fatal diagnosis, have two blankets and two outfits, one in which to bury the baby and the other to keep.

The time immediately after the birth may be the only time you will have to collect tangible memories of your child. Mementos may help in future healing and will give siblings a sense that their brother or sister really did exist.

The hand/feet molds are adorable, priceless!! But one of her right foot had a big air bubble and only got the heel! GRRR!!! We may buy one more kit and see if the mortician will try and get it for us; even if it's not how it was at birth, we'd still like to have it. I am sooooo glad Joyann made it to full term!!!! We were able to see her features and distinguishing characteristics and it was wonderful! Joyann has the characteristic crooked pinky that my mom and son, Joseph, share!!! How wonderful to know this! When the nurse took Joyann's little footprints for the hospital birth certificate, not all of her little toes showed up. The head nurse tried on three different birth certificates until she got all ten toes to show up! On her left pinky toe, she has the same thing as my hubby — her little toe is kind of sideways! Her other toes are just like mine. My hubby and I kept our angel Joyann with us for ten hours after she died. We held her the whole time and marveled at her unbelievable beauty. The nurses and even the lab techs wanted to see our baby and were so kind and loving to us. They gave us a little crocheted blanket for Joyann that she laid on and I sleep with; they gave us a memory box with a lock of her dark brown hair (like mine). Her hair was soft and fuzzy. She had hair behind her ears and I rubbed

---

3. http://www.angelfire.com/ny5/jonathandobkowski/Birthplan.html. Used with permission.

it. She had actually pretty mild anencephaly. The nurses took pictures of Joyann with a little ring on her finger that we got to keep and with a beaded bracelet in pink and blue that said BABY. They dressed her in a little T-shirt that was open in the front and a matching cap with a ball on the top. They put an extra set of the T-shirt and other memorabilia in a little purple memory box for us to take home.

*(Jewell, mom of Joyann who
was born with anencephaly)*

The hospital staff may prepare mementos for you. Ask them about this.

The nurse brought back Sydney's *The Foot Book*. Inside the front cover, they had made imprints of Sydney's little feet before they had brought her back to us. They had also taken pictures and video that we didn't know until later.

*(Heather, mom of Sydney Grace who
was born with brittle bone disease)*

How will you display photos or mementos? How will you celebrate her birthday and/or death day? Each family must decide this.

There will be no viewing of her body, because I do not wish for her to be an object of curiosity. Her picture will not be hung on our wall with our family for the same reason. We have no shame of her, but we will protect her from being degraded by others. I want to hang Sydney's photo in our bedroom. Private enough for viewing, but not public enough for the neighbor boys to ridicule her. I just cannot subject that sweet child to the cruelty of those who would despise her just for her appearance.

*(Laura, mom of Sidney who
was born with a lethal form of dwarfism)*

My husband has a big beautiful picture of Andrew. We celebrate Andrew's birthday every year. Every year we acknowledge him.

*(Emily, mom of Andrew who
was born with Trisomy 13)*

The Actual Birth

Some parents immediately bond with their babies.

All of her little things made her special to me. I didn't see Trisomy 18. I just saw my precious little girl. She wasn't the monster the doctors had painted for me — she was just a little sweetheart. All she needed was love. Boy, did she get it!

*(Christine, mom of Grace Ann
who was born with Trisomy 18)*

Some parents take a bit longer.

> When I saw Kelsey for the first time, I didn't truly feel sick, but I said to my sister, "I need to go back to my room. I'm not feeling well." I couldn't go back there. I didn't hold her for the first night. I thought what a terrible mother you are. I just couldn't handle it because it felt so, so overwhelming. She was so, so sick. I came around to being able to hold her, but it really was scary. They didn't think she would live for a day, and then two days, and then a week and then she wouldn't live for a month. And then she wouldn't live — that went on for her first three years.
>
> *(Chylene, mom of Kelsey who*
> *was born with CMTC Syndrome)*

Celebrating Life

You may have time with your child. Each moment will be a blessing.

> The biggest surprise was the incredible joy even with all the sorrow. Though she was so frail and near death, we cherished every moment, holding her in our arms the entire five days, afraid to sleep. Our other two children, Nathan (five) and Sarah (two), loved her without prejudice. The whole family gathered in the room for her first bath, and we laughed when she pooped on Grandma.
>
> *(Steve, dad of Abigail who*
> *was born with Trisomy 18)*

The Decision to Let Go

Sometimes parents have to make difficult decisions for babies who are dying.

> Sydney Grace was born September 17, 2000. She had the most lethal type of brittle bone disease. She had many fractures from being in the womb, some of which had already healed. I did get to hold Sydney about four hours after she was born. What a precious moment. Sydney was put on a respirator, but it was so hard to see her there. I was afraid to even touch her for fear of fracturing a bone. We made sure we did everything we could for her. We took lots of pictures (five rolls), two videos, sang to her, read to her, let her see her big sister, and just let her know every moment that she was so loved. The hospital staff did everything they could. There would be no miraculous recovery. On September 22, it was obvious that she was in pain. We had not noticed this before. So, even though it broke our hearts, we made the heart-wrenching decision to have her taken off the respirator. We called our families and pastor and told them to come quickly so

they could tell her goodbye. At 3:06 pm, about thirty minutes after the respirator was removed, Sydney passed away. We were allowed to stay in the room and spend as much time as we needed with her. We bathed her, dressed her, and basically just held her because we were not really able to do so while she was living. We ended up spending another five hours or so with her, although it was not really her, just her body. The hardest thing I ever had to do was hand my daughter over to the nurse, knowing I would never get to hold her on this Earth again.

(Heather, mom of Sydney Grace who
was born with brittle bone disease)

Milk Banks

Your baby may die before your milk comes in. Having the milk but not the baby can be a special torture.

As painful as it was to have my milk come in, it is now just a little disappointing to have it drying up. It's like the last bit of my body's response to Sidney is going away.

(Laura, mom of Sidney who
was born with a lethal form of dwarfism)

You may want to donate your breast milk to a milk bank. Appendix B lists contact information.

Death Plan

Making arrangements for your baby's death, before your baby is born, can be very difficult. It is wise, however, to make those plans when you have the time to think clearly. If your baby survives, you can always discard the plans.

Doran and I went to the funeral home to make arrangements. I did OK until we looked at little caskets. How horrible. They were so little. Some looked like coolers but there was one — we were told that the hospital provided that same casket free if our baby died while there. Even harder was picking out the cemetery plot. We would get two plots and Doran and I and the baby would be buried there. As we looked at plots, my baby was kicking and moving around. I had to retreat in tears to the van. I can't think of anything more horrific than planning a funeral while still feeling this little life.

(Sue, mom of Lucas Adam
who was born with anencephaly)

When Death Comes

How will you react when death comes? Try not to be afraid. Most moms and dads parent their deceased children until they feel ready to relinquish their bodies.

> We were told we could have as much time as we needed with Sydney. I asked if I could give Sydney a bath and a nurse brought the necessary supplies. She also brought materials for us to make our own footprints for Sydney. At one point I realized I had not taken Sydney to see the sunshine before she died. I started crying and Brian reminded me that she was now surrounded by sunshine. He was right. I took her over to the window anyway and asked Brian to take our picture. I also decided to give her a bath there. Brian helped bathe her and then we put lotion on her. After Kelsea takes baths, I still put lotion on her and each time the scent reminds me of Sydney. We dried her off and rocked her some more. I sang to her and read to her again. We took many pictures of us holding her. I tried to memorize every little detail about her. I ran her fingers, toes, and her hair against my lips, memorizing how they felt.
>
> *(Heather, mom of Sydney Grace who*
> *was born with brittle bone disease)*

> I do not need a doctor to know that there is no life anymore. I cry and cry, partly because I am sad but mainly because I am happy to know for certain that Anouk's soul is now with God. Christophe cries, too, and it does me good. Before washing and dressing Anouk, we take her footprints and handprints, because it is important for me to keep as many souvenirs as possible. After that, nothing keeps us at the hospital, and our children need us at home. There is neither bitterness nor lamentation and I do not regret for one second the last months. I am glad despite my sadness because "Death has been swallowed up in victory." We gave all our love to Anouk and now we can let her go.
>
> *(Monika, mom of Anouk who*
> *was born with anencephaly)*

Parenting the baby even after death brings peace and comfort.

> Lucas Adam lived for forty-five minutes. He never moved or cried but he did have his eyes open. He had my mouth and his daddy's eyes and long toes! He was beautiful and weighed four pounds ten ounces. He died peacefully in his daddy's arms. I had requested that he stay with me the night. I held him and rocked, sang lullabies he would never hear, sobbed and said my goodbyes. When I was ready I laid him down and slept the best sleep I had had in a long time. In the morning I told the doctor that I was going home. I needed to be with my family. The nurse came in with the casket. I cuddled Luke warmly into the yellow afghan I had made him, snuggled him

comfortably into his final bed and the nurse took him away forever. Doran and the kids came soon after to pick me up.

(Sue, mom of Lucas Adam who
was born with anencephaly)

After the Baby Dies

Do you want:
- To keep any stuffed toy the baby had?
- To write a letter to your baby and put it in the casket?
- To decorate the casket?
- To send birth/death announcements?
- To take photos of flowers sent to you?
- To press flowers to keep?
- To buy a special candle for the funeral and then keep it to light on birthdays and holidays?
- To make a photo album or scrapbook?
- To plant a tree or other living plant in your child's memory?
- To make a donation to charity in memory of your child?
- To write your baby's story?
- To make a memory box in which to keep your baby's mementos?
- To write a poem for your baby?

If you would like to bring your baby's body home for a time, write this into the birth plan.

I remember thinking, "Wait a minute, he isn't moving, he's mottled and blue-ish, and his cord is white. He is dead!" I did not really expect that; I never assumed he would die before being born. I had to absorb in a moment that this precious, wanted, beautiful baby was already gone. Time seemed to stop, but it was only seconds before I called for water to welcome him into Heaven through Baptism. We love him so! I caressed him, kissed him, and mothered him. Ray helped weigh Loren, bathed him, dressed him, then we took many photos of and with our son. My brother Jim came and held our boy for over an hour. The hospital priest arrived and baptized Loren again. We brought Loren home where he spent the night with us and had the chance to meet his older siblings and my sister as well as her daughter. Before driving Loren to the funeral home to make arrangements for cremation, Ray first drove Loren all around our town and neighborhood, showing him where he would've played and lived, and saying his farewell to our son.

(Ann Marie, mom of Loren
who was born with anencephaly)

Obituaries, Funerals, and Memorial Services

Some families put an obituary for their child into the newspaper. Here is Loren's obituary:

> Loren Joseph Henninger
> -Stillborn but Still Born-
>
> Our precious son Loren was born September 20th and was born again into eternal life with Jesus that same day. Welcomed tenderly into the world by his parents, Ray Loren Henninger and Ann Marie Trebon. Loved and missed by his brother, Ean, and sisters, Erin, and Kate. Thanks to family and dear friends for their love and continued support. His life has been a blessing and a miracle and he is now at peace with our Creator. Memorials may be made to the Sequim Branch of the North Olympic Library System (2210 S. Peabody, Port Angeles, WA 98362) to be used for the purchase of children's books.
>
> (Loren was born with anencephaly)[4]

If you hold a funeral or memorial service for your child, you may wish to compose a program for those attending. Here is an example of one family's program:

> Abigail Grace Wilsford
> August 27–September 1, 2002
> A Celebration of her Eternal Life:
> September 14, 2002
>
> Dear Brothers and Sisters in Christ,
> and Family and Friends:
>
> Thank you so much for coming here today to help us celebrate the eternal life of our daughter and sister, Abigail Grace Wilsford. While our hearts are broken at giving her up, we feel blessed to have had her in our lives. She has changed us forever, and we want to share with you both our sorrow and joy. We also wanted to tell you a bit about Abigail's story up until this day....
>
> (Steven and Mindy, parents of Abigail Grace,
born with Trisomy 18)[5]

Here are excerpts from a funeral bulletin which also requested charitable donations in lieu of flowers:

> To all of our family and friends:
> We want to thank each of you for your unending prayers, support and compassion you have given us during this difficult time.

---

4. See http://www.geocities.com/simonmanz/friend.html. Used with permission.

5. See http://www.geocities.com/wilsfordmindy/Abby_Letter. Used with permission.

We could not have gotten through this on our own. We have learned a lot along the way, especially about God's presence in our lives. We feel truly blessed to have our three beautiful healthy children and we feel Jonathan Steven will now be our guardian angel. We thank God for each of you and pray that God will bless you all.

A special thank you to Sister Pat; without her guidance and support, we would not have been able to endure the daily struggles.

Another special thank you to Mary Gravina from Hospice. She has taught us how to deal gracefully with difficult issues with our children in an open and honest manner.

Donations can be made in the name of Jonathan Steven Dobkowski to:

Hospice Care Network
14 Shore Lane
Bay Shore, NY 11706
c/o Mary Gravina
God bless you,

Donna and Walter Dobkowski (from the funeral bulletin for Jonathan Dobkowski who was born with Potter's Syndrome)[6]

Some families have a public, social gathering after the funeral or memorial service.

We spent the week after Loren's death planning a funeral liturgy. We chose the reading, readers, prayers of the faithful, music, and poetry we would read. This celebration of Loren's life was held in our church, with a potluck luncheon following at our home.

(Ann Marie, mom of Loren who was born with anencephaly)

Some families do not want a large, public service.

We have decided not to have a funeral. Those who did know her are grieving her loss, and in no condition to speak, and a public event is not something I can bear now.

(Laura, mom of Sidney who was born with a lethal form of dwarfism)

We buried Luke on a bright sunny day. We had a family-only graveside service. The kids let off balloons to go to heaven for Luke. They had a great time competing to see whose would get there first! Then it was done, except it still isn't a year later. Luke left us for another place, but he is still with us. He brought us so much.

(Sue, mom of Lucas Adam who was born with anencephaly)

---

6. See http://www.angelfire.com/ny5/jonathandobkowski/JonathansFuneral.html. Used with permission.

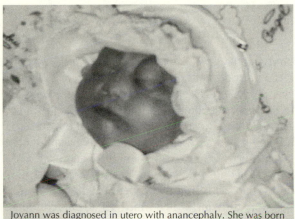

Joyann was diagnosed in utero with anancephaly. She was born at full term but lived only four minutes. Hospital staff allowed her parents to keep Joyann's body with them until they felt ready to release her to the hospital ten hours after her death.

Grief

The strength of your grief may startle you. You grieve because you love. You grieve not only the immediate loss of your child but also your future with him or her.

> Today I miss her very much. The other kids help, but do not replace that intense need which a newborn would have. That is the difference in grieving between a mother and a father. The mother is constantly aware of the presence of the baby, the father is not. He notices and pays attention when the baby requires attention. When an infant dies, the mother is constantly aware of the baby's absence, as though a part of herself were missing. The father may be affected by the loss only when he thinks about it. The loss is different to each.
>
> *(Laura, mom of Sidney who*
> *was born with a lethal form of dwarfism)*

You may experience any or all of these reactions:

- Preoccupation with thoughts of the baby.

- Heightened impatience, frustration, lack of direction, indecisiveness, fear, despair, worry, yearning for comfort, anger, carelessness, numbness, guilt, resentment toward others.

- Physical problems such as difficulty breathing, sleeplessness, fatigue, depression, spontaneous crying, feeling empty, appetite changes, tightness in the throat, racing heartbeat.

- Obsessions with cleaning, health, well-being of other children or spouse, work, cleanliness, food, exercise, harmful substances such as drugs or alcohol.

You can have these reactions if your baby is stillborn or if he lives for a while and then dies.

> Surviving the loss of my Karlee Rose [*at the age of two years*] has been the most difficult time of my life. It's just plain hard work. And it never goes away. The pain (excruciating) is always there. Time does make that pain not come to the surface as often. Brad and I cried, and prayed and talked (just like when we found out about her birth defect) and cried. I read tons of books on the loss of a child. I found an internet web ring called "Empty Arms" and read, and read, and read. It helped to know I was not the only one to lose a child. I joined an internet support group, and Brad and I went to grief counseling. The "firsts" were so very difficult — first time back to church (ouch!), first time to the hairdresser, dentist, grocery store (another ouch), back to school.
>
> *(Katie, mom of Karlee Rose, Benal, and Nikki,*
> *all of whom were born with spina bifida)*

The persistence of grief may surprise you. At unexpected moments, memories may spring up and tears flow. One mother compared her seven-year grief journey to a roller coaster ride. You never know where the peaks, dips, and curves are, but you know that they exist, that they will suddenly be upon you, and that you will hang on for dear life when you encounter them. You also know you will survive the ride and, at some point, climb off.[7] Let the tears flow as often and as intensely as they come. Do not fight grief, but let it carry you along like a wave until its power abates. There is healing in the tears.

> At times my arms ached so much I couldn't use them. I thought I was losing my mind and my faith. The pain of mourning, the loss of a child, I don't think can be compared. We know that truth is absolute, because God is truth. We must be made into His image, not He into ours. To follow the same path that He walked. What immeasurable glory, that He would raise my human dignity to follow His path of suffering and so to be made into His likeness. What similarities to Our Lady's suffering! I glimpse the extent of her love for God and for us.
>
> *(Jeanne, mom of Maria G. who*
> *was born with Trisomy 18)*

Certain dates and anniversaries can be especially difficult. Make plans for those dates. Invite friends over or decide to do something special. You may wish to share this essay with others:

---

7. Susan Helling, "The Ride," in *You Will Dream New Dreams*, 201–4.

Grieving

My baby died. It is the most tragic thing that has happened in my life. I know it makes you uncomfortable. I know you want to help. Please try, but do not try to fix me.

Share your faith with me. It helps mine be stronger, but do not try to tell me how I should feel if I really believe. Believing, even knowing, does not remove grief.

Do not tell me there is hope in Jesus and expect it to take away the pain. I know the doctrine — it offers me great comfort and it helps me endure, but does not replace the presence of my beloved child.

Do not tell me that I will see my child again as though I have forgotten in my grief. I know that, but it does not make me miss her less now or take away the loneliness.

Do not belittle the short time she had as though she had no power to touch others. Her life has greater meaning than those minutes and her mission reached beyond her own life.

Do not tell me she was perfect as though the honor of having a perfect child should compensate for her absence. I know she was perfect, I felt her.

Do not try to comfort me by telling me it would have been hard to care for her with the problems she had. I loved and wanted her anyway and I was willing to face any hardship for her.

And please do not tell me she is happier now as though I should be glad to let her go. It is the absence of her joyful spirit that leaves such a void now.

It is the motive behind your words that makes them appropriate or not. I can feel when you love me, or when you are trying to educate me out of my loss.

Please do not ignore my loss and avoid me. Please have the courage to ask me how I am, even if you fear my tears. You don't have to know what to say, I will understand. I just want to know you care.

Please tell me you are sorry, or that you would like to take away my pain if you could.

Tell me you love me and would have liked to know my child. It may cause me pain if you mention her name but I need you to do so, because it will also offer me the comfort that someone other than just me remembers her, and I need to know that. Fumbling words from a sincere heart mean more to me than trite phrases that sound good on the surface.

If you tell me that I can call you if I need anything, I won't do it. I may not be capable of asking for help when I need it most, or I may not be able to ask for what I really need.

If you offer something and I do not want it today, I may need it tomorrow, so please do not be offended if I refuse your offer. My feelings change frequently, and sometimes I may not even know what it is I need. I appreciate it so much when someone truly listens to the Holy Spirit and performs a kind and thoughtful act.

If I feel anger at God, it does not mean I lost my faith. It just means this is so big and so heartbreaking that I do not understand why the Lord let it happen the way it did. But I will in time. I know He has a plan for me and this will work for my good. I am still confused and hurt that it happened, but I still have faith. I know there are blessings in this, I have felt them. I know they were worth it, but I still hurt.

Please bring meals or flowers if you want to. They are a tangible reminder that someone cared enough to take time to try to comfort me. But also stop to listen so I know it is more than just a gesture.

And give me the time I need — it might be much longer than you think. Do not try to rush me through to being OK again.

Do not try to fix me. I am not broken. I am only grieving. Just love me, and I will survive.

*(Laura Wheeler, mom of Sidney who
was born with lethal dwarfism)*[8]

Mystical Experience

Some parents experience something mystical after their child's death.

I remember every single detail about the morning that Karlee died. It was horrible, tragic. BUT there was one moment that was magical. When they finally let me in the emergency room, she had already passed. I was alone with her. Her spirit was there in the room. I felt her and she was at peace, happy, joyful. She was floating above us and happy. She was getting ready to watch *Blue's Clues*, her favorite show. And I had an insane peaceful feeling that she was safe. Nothing more could cause her pain. She was where she needed to be. Then, in a flash, her spirit was gone.

*(Katie, mom of Karlee Rose, Benal, and Nikki,
all of whom were born with spina bifidia)*

That night after Lucas Adam died, I woke out of a sound sleep. One of the kids was standing by my bed and needed something. This happened often. Whoever it was would stand there looking at me until I woke up. For some reason they never touched me and I usually woke up before they spoke so this night was no different than usual. I rolled over and no one was there, yet someone was. I felt him. I think Luke came to tell me he was OK. Then he was gone.

*(Sue, mom of Lucas Adam who
was born with anencephaly)*

---

8. Reprinted with permission from *Carrying to Term with a Negative Prenatal Diagnosis*, http://www.sidneyfaith.ws/sidney/grief.htm, © 2005.

In the past five weeks since Maria's entrance into Paradise, I've often wondered, How do the children in Heaven spend their days? Do they run, jump and play as children on earth or do they spend all of their time adoring the most Holy and Blessed Trinity? So, I asked Our Lord if He would give me a sign; some indication that Maria was okay, in Heaven and happy. A couple of weeks passed, and I received a phone call for my husband from someone I didn't know. During our conversation, the woman happened to mention a dream that her twelve-year-old daughter, Holly, had recently. Holly dreamed that she went to Heaven. There were rainbows everywhere with puffy clouds, a big gate and Jesus and Mary were there sitting on thrones that were made of clouds. And there were babies everywhere sliding down the rainbows! I burst into tears of ecstasy. Thank you, Jesus! My little girl is okay, she is blessed, she is bounteous in Heaven with all of the other babies who have moved on. And she is running, jumping and sliding down rainbows all the day long!

(Terri, mom of Maria D. who was born with spina bifida and fatal physical conditions)

Siblings and Grief

If you have other children and your new baby has a fatal condition, you will have to deal with your children's grief. Here are some suggestions:

- Be honest with your children.

- Use age-appropriate language to help children understand what is happening.

- Listen to their fears, hurts, anger, and concerns.

- Learn to use words that encourage them to talk about their feelings:
  "How does that make you feel?"
  "Do you want to talk about it?"
  "Is there anything I can do to help you feel better?"
  "Thank you for telling me that. You are a very brave person."
  "I know you are hurting, but I am always here for you."
  "It is OK to cry."

- Help children say goodbye to their brother or sister: write a letter, draw a picture, write a poem, or make something for the funeral.

We also encouraged [our other children] to make or to select something special to place in the casket from them. My mom found a boy's white and blue sleeper that actually had wings and said "Angel Baby" on it.

(Sue, mom of Lucas Adam who was born with anencephaly)

ℒ Celebrate the memory of their sibling: plant a tree, make a special garden, donate to a charity, make a scrapbook of memories, blow bubbles on a windy hill, or fly a kite with the baby's name attached to the string.

ℒ Keep the baby's picture in a place of honor.

ℒ Talk about their brother or sister on special days, such as their sibling's birthday. You might even have a birthday party.

ℒ Laugh and remember the good times together.[9]

Other People

People may expect you to get "back to normal" especially if your baby did not survive very long.

> I answered the phone, and his mother asked me how I was doing, then cheerfully said, "Well, it's back to life as usual for you then!" I called Kevin to the phone because I just could not talk to her. No, it is not back to life as usual. I am forever changed. Normality will come back in a different form than before.
>
> *(Laura, mom of Sidney who was*
> *born with a lethal form of dwarfism)*

Try to find people who will support you wherever you are in your grief journey.

> It's good to know that others are out there who survived it. After Casey died, when people started to find out, a lot of people told me that they had experienced something similar. Talking to those people was the biggest help. The ones who had been through the same thing got me through it. You think you will never feel joy again. When you start to feel better, you feel guilty. You get over that.
>
> *(Sandy, mom of Casey who*
> *was born with Trisomy 18)*

What do you say if people ask how many children you have? Do you include your baby who died or not?

Each parent must come to his or her own solution to this problem. Here are some possible answers to the question:

ℒ "We have five kids, three here and two in heaven."

ℒ "We have one child but she is with God."

ℒ "Our first baby died. Thanks for asking."

---

9. Adapted from Susan Titus Osborn and Janet Lynn Mitchell, *A Special Kind of Love: For Those Who Love Children with Special Needs* (Nashville, Tennessee: Broadman and Holman Publishers, 2003), 142.

Nancy Halco has three living children and two who have died. Her living children figured out how to respond when someone asks Nancy, "How many children do you have?" She replies, "Three down and two up."

Who Are You?

Children whose parents have died are called orphans. Spouses whose spouse has died are called widowers or widows. What should you be called if your baby dies, before or after birth?

How about claiming the title of parent?

> [P]arents with a child in Heaven are still mothers and fathers, and they have the challenge of grieving and loving and cherishing a child from a most painful distance. I remember reading a wonderful quote from a Catholic mother who said we do not have our children for this life; we have them for the life to come. Whether our children are safe with us or resting in the arms of God, we are still their mothers and fathers and they remain our precious babes.[10]

> We still call ourselves Nathan's mother and father, and, although sometimes that might cause discomfort on the part of the person we're talking with, it's important for them to see us as his parents. I say, "I've had three children. Emilie is twenty-six, Matthew is twenty-one, and our middle child, Nathan, died of a rare genetic disease at the age of fourteen."
>
> *(Jennifer, mom of Nathan who*
> *was born with Menke's Disease)*

Healing

Mothers and fathers heal at different rates. Try to be patient with your spouse's timetable.

> Another unforeseen blessing is the drawing together of our family. I love my wife a little more. I love my children a little more. I hug them all a little more tightly and a little more often. I love my family, friends, and neighbors, even strangers a little more. I cherish my very short time on the earth a little more. And I'm much more careful to make my salvation sure so that I can see Abigail Grace again soon. All this is by choice. Be patient, especially with your wife. What is ahead is a battle of sorts. Fight uncertainty with knowledge. Fight sorrow with joy, Fight bitterness with love.
>
> *(Steve, dad of Abigail who*
> *was born with Trisomy 18)*

Your spouse can help in the healing, just by being there.

---

10.   Tracy Webb, Elizabeth Ministries (personal email to author, 14 April 2005).

When I was holding Kevin's hand in Wal-Mart I told him, "I have no baby to hold, so you will have to substitute!" I meant it jokingly, but it has some truth. Having extra time and comfort from those I am closest to helps fill the gap some. And Kevin is the one I need it from most.

(Laura, mom of Sidney who was
born with a lethal form of dwarfism)

Healing takes time, but it does come.

Our spiritual faith has been unbelievably strengthened. We have learned the true meaning of unconditional love. I, personally, have learned who is REALLY in control and it is not me! I can accept anything and I can accomplish anything. Our kids know we will sacrifice anything for them. I have found a true community of faith in our church. I will never be able to repay all the people who supported us and accepted Luke despite his diagnosis. These people never saw Luke or felt him but still supported him through me.

(Sue, mom of Lucas Adam who
was born with anencephaly)

One way to foster healing is by doing something good for others.

After Gianna was born and died, my emotions came to a standstill. Instead of taking the time to grieve, I ran headlong into the busyness of life. Not wanting to go to a quiet place and cry, I carried myself into a depression. My doctor was very supportive and first recommended counseling and then my volunteering at a free clinic. By reaching out to other people, I was able to begin the healing process. Instead of escaping, I allowed God to lead me. Each day I place myself in His hands, asking Him to send signals loud enough that I may respond in order to assist someone in need.

(Doreen, mom of Gianna who was born with Trisomy 13 and
holoprosencephaly)

I learned that I just cannot participate in the decision-making boards [*internet forums for parents who are deciding whether or not to continue a pregnancy*]; it is too hard. It makes me physically ill to do so. So, as Sidney's legacy, I built a website on Carrying to Term at http://sidneyfaith.ws/sidney/.

(Laura, mom of Sidney who was
born with a lethal form of dwarfism)

Faith in an eternal afterlife helps many families to heal.

The only way we are getting through this is with the knowledge that we will definitely see our daughter again. We will be able to hold her and kiss her and not have to worry about hurting her. She will get to meet her two baby brothers who have done so much to heal our hearts, and see her big sister again. Our family will finally once again be whole and there will be no more goodbyes.

(Heather, mom of Sydney Grace who was born with brittle bone disease)

Our job as parents is to get our kids into heaven, and I have one up there.

(Sandy, mom of Casey who was born with Trisomy 18)

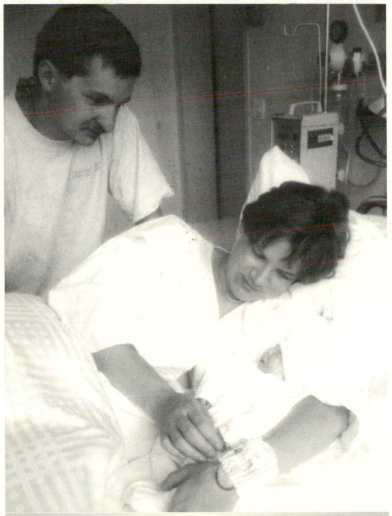

Anouk was diagnosed in utero with anencephaly. The thirteen hours of her life after birth were spent in loving visits from her siblings and grandparents. She died in her parents' arms.

7

If Your Child Lives

My basic principle is that you don't make decisions because they are easy; you don't make them because they are cheap; you don't make them because they're popular; you make them because they're right.

Theodore Hesburgh[1]

For My Brother Ben

Blessings arrive in so many ways —
A cool breeze on a hot summer's day,
A laugh, a smile, a quiet retreat,
The feel of the earth beneath your feet.
They come packaged in the form of a safe journey home,
And in knowing that you're never truly alone.
But of all these, gifts from above,
The most amazing is pure and faith-filled love.
It inspires us, moves us, gives us hope,
And is not a raft, but is a boat.
Its allies are truth and lessons learned,
And knowing some things can't be earned.
Love is more than a word, it lies in proof,
Perfect examples live under my roof.

Michelle L. Boisot, age eighteen, sister of Ben
who was born with multiple disabilities

Living with a child with differences brings both challenges and rewards. You will learn how to parent by being a parent. Your child will teach you skills no other child can teach.

We had a lot to learn about caring for a "heart baby" — but, all in all, it was not very difficult. There were feeding issues and we had to rent an oximeter to occasionally monitor her oxygen saturation levels. All of this I learned how to do quickly. Even though our insurance provided home nursing, I cancelled it, because there was nothing that the nurses did that I couldn't do, and I have no formal medical training whatsoever.

(Monica, mom of Celine who was born
with hypoplastic right heart syndrome)

---

1. http://www.whatquote.com/quotes/Theodore-M--Hesburgh/37078-My-basic-principle-i.htm.

Your journey can be easier when you learn from those who have walked similar roads. This chapter and the next will share some of these parents' insights.

> For a while I heard a lot of stories on TV, etc. about how hard it was to give birth to a child with disabilities and therefore abortion needs to be legalized to prevent that anguish. I would always talk back to the TV and say, "But you don't ask ME if it's hard — ask some parents."
>
> *(Jennifer, mom of Nathan who*
> *was born with Menke's Disease)*

Dealing with Yourself

The first person to deal with is yourself. If your child faces serious surgeries, you may be very anxious until they are over.

> The first week is a blur in my memory. I can recall the events very well, but I was a wreck. When one of the senior cardiologists entered the hospital room with some residents, I had to ask them to forgive me for being unable to stop sobbing, and assured him to keep talking, I was listening. Frankly, I was a basket case for the entire three weeks that Celine was hospitalized with her first surgery. She, on the other hand, did very well!
>
> *(Monica, mom of Celine who was born*
> *with hypoplastic right heart syndrome)*

Much has to do with attitude. You have suffered losses and disappointments. How do you want to live from now on? If you decide to be positive, you will be. If you want to wallow in self-pity, you will. No matter what happens with your child, you are responsible for your own emotional healing.

> I can remember every doctor's appointment, CAT scan, MRI, shunt tap, every drop of blood taken from his body, testing for all sorts of things, the smell of the hospitals, the smell of the medicines, the sounds of the machines, the sound of the doctor's shoes as he walked towards Nick's hospital bed, the pale look of Nick's skin after major surgeries, the feeling of total vulnerability that I have felt seeing my son hooked up to every conceivable machine keeping him stabilized, the total helplessness, knowing that I could do nothing to help him with the pain. As the mother of a child with a disability I can honestly tell another parent there is a pain that never disappears. It doesn't ease as I foolishly convinced myself early on that it would. You learn to deal with it; you learn ways in which to cope. You learn to be strong when others are falling apart, when others can't seem to lift themselves out of sorrow. You learn that with time this surgery or this issue will resolve itself and pass.
>
> *(Ashley, mom of Nick who*
> *was born with spina bifida)*

Your emotions may surprise you. No matter how much you love your child, you may sometimes find yourself angry, resentful, or bitter for having a child with such differences. Talk about these perfectly normal emotions with someone who can understand. Try to get to the root of your feelings.

Parents often discover that they need to forgive someone:

- ❧ Spouse?
- ❧ Friends?
- ❧ Family?
- ❧ Their child?
- ❧ Strangers?
- ❧ Doctors?
- ❧ Themselves?
- ❧ God?

Nick was born with spina bifida. He hopes to become a veterinarian.

Forgiveness means disconnecting the replay button on distressing incidents and moving on. Lewis B. Smedes, professor emeritus of theology and ethics at Fuller Theological Seminary, wrote, "To forgive is to set a prisoner free, and discover that the prisoner was you."[2] Only as you leave behind negative emotions will you be able to deal successfully with the future.

You might wish your child would die or wonder if you did the right thing in giving birth or seeking treatment.

> I remember at my lowest point, when he was around three, and getting one diagnosis after another and the list of specialists was getting longer and longer. I made my husband take time off from work to go to an appointment because I just couldn't bear to hear someone else tell me there was something else wrong with Alex. At that point I really wondered if I did right by him by asking for heroic measures in the NICU. The thing that pulled me through was separating what my feelings were from how Alex acted. He has always been very easygoing and interactive and happy. I was the one who was having trouble handling his medical issues.
>
> *(Joanne, mom of Alex who*
> *has multiple disabilities)*

---

2. http://www.quotiki.com/quote.aspx?id=10026.

Make a list of things you feel guilty about. Talk over the list with another person. Cross off the ones you are not responsible for. Cross off the ones you cannot change. Make a plan of action for dealing with the rest.[3] Remember that you did not cause your child's condition. You made the best decisions possible. You are doing the best you can now. Guilt saps strength and hope. Say goodbye to guilt forever.

Promise to relax. You are not Super-parent. You cannot control everything, and you are not responsible for everything. Make a list of what is important to you. Then order the items from most to least important. Work on the top priorities. You may need to let the others slip. Dorothy Day, a social activist, once advised a bride, "Lower your standards," since she could not meet the ones she had set.[4]

Simplify your life. Where do you really have to go? What really needs to be done? If you have less to achieve, you will be more successful at accomplishing it.

Try to avoid the "am I doing the best for my child?" morass. Obsessively searching for another treatment, educational plan, surgery, doctor, diet, or exercise can sap your energy and prevent you from accepting your child as she is.

> We had people who said, "If you go out to Washington State, you can find this doctor, and if you go out here, you can find this doctor." And we just had to say, "We've gone to a lot of doctors. We've done what we could do. We have to accept." Kelsey enjoys life so much, and she helps us to enjoy it. That sense of humor!
>
> *(Chylene, mom of Kelsey who*
> *was born with CMTC Syndrome)*

While planning ahead is good, try not to project today's difficulties onto the future. That only causes worry. Things often change anyway.

Keep a diary. Write down problems and how you met them. As you look back, you will see that you were able to weather crises. That will give you hope in future difficulties.

Do not isolate yourself. Get out into the world with your child.

> He was a child people remembered. We took Joey to church and wherever we went, and people were very friendly. They would come over and want to see Joey. We have seven kids but the others never elicited this reaction. People would say, "Oh, how is your baby doing?" He was unforgettable.
>
> *(Erin, mom of Joey who*
> *was born with Trisomy 18)*

---

3. Simons, 13.

4. Nancy Forest Kidd, "Letter to a Bride: Side Bar," in Jim Forest, "Dorothy Day: Saint and Troublemaker," lecture given at the Dorothy Day Conference, Marquette University, Milwaukee, Wisconsin (10 October 1997). See http://www.incommunion. org/forest-flier/jimsessays/dorothy-day-saint-and-troublemaker/.

You may have to face continual problems and adjustments. You will learn to keep going. Count the successes and focus on the joys.

> We learned how to tube feed Gracie and do everything for her. She would occasionally stop breathing and she had some seizure activity. We worked closely with hospice to arrange bringing her home. I chickened out about two weeks into it — she had a severe seizure and they were about to pronounce her gone. I thought, "Hell, I can't do this in my living room with my kids — am I crazy?" But, two weeks later we got used to it. We brought her home on her one-month birthday. That was a great day!
>
> *(Christine, mom of Grace Ann*
> *who was born with Trisomy 18)*

Meet Your Own Needs

Caring for your child can become all-consuming. You need time to yourself. List your needs and plan to meet them. Who can help you? How? Here are some suggestions to help you maintain strength and perspective so that you can continue to be a good parent:

- Make a date with your spouse.
- Hire a babysitter and take a long, leisurely bath.
- At least once daily, spend fifteen minutes doing something you like. Find someone to watch your child during that time.
- Attend a mothers' group, weekly if possible. You could take your child along.

> My husband started sending me out on Saturdays when he was home to do whatever I wanted for awhile. After the other two children were in school, Nathan was portable, so we went to book stores, craft stores, etc., together. He liked going out, and I think it was good for him socially. I know it was good for me! Another way I got "me" time was late at night, after everyone was asleep. Often Nathan would still be wide awake at midnight or later. I couldn't sleep until he was asleep, so I used those late night hours for me — I'm an artist, so I did a LOT of my artwork in the wee hours. He'd lie there and watch me and eventually drift off to sleep.
>
> *(Jennifer, mom of Nathan who was born with Menke's Disease)*

Support Groups and Agencies

Other parents of children with differences can offer much support and insight.

I'd been looking on the internet for a support group. I just wasn't finding it. Suddenly I met someone who introduced me to an internet group for parents of children with disabilities, called Our-Kids. I'd never found anything that exactly matched our situation, and then suddenly there it was — a group of parents of children, mostly severely disabled, all dealing with many of the same issues! That group now numbers around eight hundred families. I still stay very actively involved.

(Jennifer, mom of Nathan who
was born with Menke's Disease)

Associate with local support groups for children with the same or similar condition as yours. If you cannot find such a group, start one. The acceptance level in such groups is incredible.

We went to a race for children with limb differences. It is the only place I've been to where there were thousands of people and nobody stared because everyone there was familiar with limb differences.

(Patricia, mom of Jessica who was born
with limb differences of both arms and both legs)

Ciarra has changed me so much. I sure have slowed down to enjoy the world more. She is perpetually hopeful, and most often smiling. She is the closest thing to an angel as I will ever see. Through her, I have started an online support group. We are a close-knit community. Several of our members are moms I tried to lend a little hope to when I found them shortly after their diagnosis.

(Michelle, mom of Ciarra who
was born with Down syndrome)

Use the internet, ask your physician, or contact state or local agencies about helpful groups. Spend time, via internet or phone, researching agencies that might provide the services and information you need. Often one contact will lead to another. Here is the question to ask:

"My child (include the child's name) has _____ (name condition and describe). I am looking for agencies that may assist us in meeting his (her) needs as well as parent support groups. Can you make a referral?"

If the agency says they do not know of any referrals, ask:

"Can you refer me to someone who may know?"

Keep an alphabetized list, either on file cards or in a computer file, of those you have called, whether you left a phone message, when you called back, the result of the phone call, and so on. Put unhelpful agencies into their own group. If you have to call again, you will know which agencies were able to assist you and which were not.

We took advantage of First Steps — a program for kids with special-needs. Did physical, occupational, and speech therapy with Karlee. Later enrolled her in special-needs preschool. She got her first wheelchair and this was the best thing we did for her. It allowed her to sit up (she had low muscle tone) and be at her peers' level. She blossomed! She was very verbal and very smart. She learned to count in Spanish!

(Katie, mom of Karlee Rose, Benal, and Nikki,
all of whom were born with spina bifida)

Generally families are able to care for their children. However, neighbors, family members, friends, and agencies can assist.

Nathan and I spent fourteen years living almost symbiotically. He was dependent for all of his needs, and I met those needs willingly and eagerly. My husband and I did all his care, only very occasionally getting a nurse for him. As our other two children grew older, they were involved with Nathan's care as well.

(Jennifer, mom of Nathan who
was born with Menke's Disease)

Find out what governmental help is available and what laws can assist you. If no legislation exists, work for some.

Respect Your Child

Your child is more like other children than unlike them. Respect your daughter as a human being. Avoid talking about your son's "problems" within his hearing. Your child ought not think of herself or himself as a "problem." If someone asks you about your son's condition in his presence, think of a positive, stock answer. Use his name and address him when you speak. People First Language helps.

Example:

"What is wrong with him?"

Answer: "Nothing is wrong with Wayne. You, Wayne, are a terrific son!"

"Oh, I mean why is he in a stroller? He seems so big."

Answer: "Oh, that! Wayne, you think the stroller is great, right? If you did not have spina bifida, you would have to walk around this store like me and be bored silly. But now you get to ride like the wind!"

When you discuss your child with others, focus on her abilities and achievements, not her disability or diagnosis. How you discuss your child has a great influence on how others think of her. More importantly, it influences how your child thinks of herself. Do you want your child to think of herself as a burden to you or as a gift? A child's diagnosis is best kept as private as possible, but her assets can be proclaimed to the world. Assets are not necessarily things a doctor, guidance counselor, or psychologist would list. They are traits that make your child wonderful.

As soon as your daughter can speak up for herself, teach her to do so. She will have to learn this sooner or later.

Example:

"What is wrong with her?"

Child: "Are you talking about me? Nothing is wrong with me, is there, Mom? I am in this stroller because I have spina bifida and I cannot walk very fast in the store. Nothing wrong with that, is there?"

Teach your child how to ask for, not demand, help. Children need to know that parents are not mind readers nor are they slaves or robots. Parents have intelligence and feelings, and both need to be respected. When your child asks for help, respond lovingly and patiently. If the child can do the task for himself, politely tell him so. If it is something you need to do, perform the task with joy.

> My five-year-old Alexandra was born with a clubfoot. We found out from an ultrasound when I was twenty weeks pregnant. She had four surgeries to help correct her foot. Whenever anyone asks if she broke her foot, she matter-of-factly tells them, "No. I was born with a clubfoot." She is not ashamed or embarrassed. She is in gymnastics and doing great. I have never made a big deal or acted like she was any different than any other child. I think that has made a huge impact on how she handles the situation. If I made a big deal, I believe she would, too.
>
> *(Sabra, Alexandra's mom)*

Build your child's self-esteem. Include him in all you do. Let your child — not you — set limits on what she can do. Allow your child to fail. Challenge him to reach farther. Enjoy the successes and learn from the failures.

Explaining to Others

You will want to explain your child's condition to family and friends. Invite them over and teach them how to respond to your child. Keep them updated on your child's progress. One mother wrote a letter to friends, family, coworkers, and neighbors and gave the address of a foundation that researches cures and treatments for her child's condition.

If you receive a great deal of unsolicited advice, let people know that this is your child, not theirs, and that you are in control. You may often find yourself saying, "Thanks for the advice. That's very interesting." A noncommittal response can avoid a confrontation.

How do you handle questions from strangers and acquaintances? You may not want to answer some of these questions. Make a list of common questions and write down your responses. Memorize the responses so they are on the tip of your tongue.

One family designed a small business card that explained what they wanted strangers to know. The card read:

> YOU HAVE JUST ENCOUNTERED a person with an autism spectrum disorder. He may be acting in an unusual way. Please be understanding! Autism is a developmental disorder that prevents individuals from behaving in a typical manner. http://www.autism-society.org[5]

Would you want to design a similar card for your child? Sometimes you have to educate people on the spot.

> People have a hard time understanding that she's a person. They pretend we're not there because they don't know what to do. You see mothers telling their kids, "Don't look. Don't stare." And you wonder why. You think if they would just come over and say Hi. If I can get someone's attention, I'll smile and say hello to people and they'll relax. Little kids will be very interested in Kelsey's wheelchair or her walker and want to touch it and mothers will be, "Ahhh — don't touch!" And I will say, "Kelsey doesn't mind. She likes to share."

> *(Chylene, mom of Kelsey who*
> *was born with CMTC Syndrome)*

You Say You Want to Help?

Some people will say, "What can I do? I want to help." You may feel uneasy asking someone to do something specific. How about creating a list of ways to help and handing it to those who ask?

Ways You Can Help

> Thanks so much for offering to help us. It means so much. Here are some ways you can help. Would you like to pick one and let us know what day you can help?

꙳ Wash the baby's bottles.

꙳ Do the laundry.

꙳ Make a meal.

---

5.   Susan Titus Osborn and Janet Lynn Mitchell, *A Special Kind of Love: For Those Who Love Children with Special Needs* (Nashville, Tennessee: Broadman and Holman Publishers, 2004), 43.

- ❧ Babysit the other children.
- ❧ Drive our child to an appointment or practice.
- ❧ Write thank-you notes.
- ❧ Vacuum.
- ❧ Clean the bathroom.
- ❧ Wash the kitchen floor.
- ❧ Come and sit with our child while we go out for a few hours.
- ❧ Repair the _____ (fill in the blank).
- ❧ Do our grocery shopping. We will give you a list and the money.
- ❧ Do our Christmas shopping. We will give you the list and the money.
- ❧ Cut the grass.
- ❧ Weed the garden.
- ❧ Freeze (or can) the vegetables.
- ❧ Take our children to the park (zoo, fair, museum).

Dominoes

One mother described dealing with her child's various medical crises as "watching a line of dominoes tumble, one after another."[6] Crisis may follow on the heels of crisis, and diagnosis supplant diagnosis. Eventually the dominoes stop falling, and life assumes a calmer pace. This same mom reminded herself. "It's the journey that counts, not the destination. Sometimes it's a bumpy ride; other times, it's very smooth. But it's always interesting. And, most importantly, it's a journey that John, David, and I are taking together."[7]

> Being a new parent of a kid with special needs has to be one of the hardest things I've ever gone through. Alex has multiple disabilities and one medical problem would take the spotlight, and we'd put out that fire and something new would crop up, and I'd have to learn a whole new ball game as well as trust my own instinct and common sense. It really helps to know that there is a light at the end of what seems a very long tunnel. Not sure if things actually get better or we just get used to dealing with it or a combination of both.
>
> *(Joanne, mom of Alex who*
> *was born with multiple disabilities)*

---

6. Jillian K. Welch, "The Journey," in *You Will Dream New Dreams*, 198.

7. Ibid.

Early Intervention

Early intervention, which involves physical and mental stimulation geared to your child, may help your child meet her potential. Ask your pediatrician or hospital for referrals. National organizations dealing with your child's needs may be able to advise you on techniques you can use at home. Also contact a local government official regarding laws and government agencies that can help your child. Early intervention centers support parents through groups and meetings. Continue to phone agencies and individuals until you get the information you need. The goal is to help YOUR child become what HE can become.

> We belong to the Touch of Love group, which has about thirty other kids besides Marissa who have congenital limb differences. We met lots of kids with hands like hers and we could see how other families dealt with that. Inspirational speakers, who are adults with prostheses or congenital amputations, come and share with the group.
>
> *(Mary, mom of Marissa who was born*
> *without a left hand due to amniotic band syndrome)*

Sometimes dealing with the system is more difficult and frustrating than dealing with your child. What services do you really need? If getting to or paying for parent support groups, intervention sessions, play groups, and exercise classes is causing stress and disruption, step back and evaluate whether everything you are doing is really necessary. Is what your child gaining worth the price? Can you do something at home, on your own time, to achieve the same results?

Assistive Technology

In obtaining what will help your child, ask, "What is the goal? How can the goal be reached?" Think creatively. By trying to make your child "fit" into society, you may be approaching life from the wrong angle. Maybe society needs to "fit" your child. Your child may reach goals differently than other youngsters do. For example, you may want your child to be mobile. Does this mean that your child has to learn to walk? Maybe. Maybe not. Mobility might involve motorized wheelchairs more than strengthening weak muscles.

Imagine a technological device that would help. What would this device do? How might it look? You do not have to know how to build it or where to get it. Just think about who might be able to provide this device or something like it. Where might you find these people?

Check with:

- Government agencies that deal with people with disabilities.
- The internet.
- Agencies devoted to research and education on your child's condition.
- Computer department heads at colleges and universities.
- Companies that provide assistive technology.
- Children's hospitals and medical centers.
- Mechanics.
- Carpenters.
- Electricians.
- Those who are knowledgeable about computers.
- Engineers.
- College and university professors and students in engineering, rehabilitation, education.

Someone may be able to design and construct what your child needs. If this can help your child, maybe it can help someone else, too.

> Figure skating has been my favorite. My father used an example provided by the War Amps to create a walker out of welded steel and hockey sticks, so that it could slide across the ice while providing me with support as I learned to skate.
>
> *(Stacy, an adult who was born with amniotic band syndrome which resulted in the disfigurement of her left hand and an above knee amputation)*

Presume that your child will become competent in using the technology. The goal is to meet your child's needs.

> Marissa has both a passive and an electrical prosthesis. She uses the passive one for ballet and the electrical one for theater and normal functioning which requires tying of shoes and picking things up, all of which she can do.
>
> *(Mary, mom of Marissa who was born without a left hand due to amniotic band syndrome)*

Medical Opinions and Other Diagnoses

If your child needs treatment or develops new symptoms, get a few medical opinions regarding treatment. Be assertive and ask for pros and cons regarding every treatment option.

Be sure that specialists have access to previous records and assessments including the most recent ones. Let them know if symptoms or circumstances have changed since the last assessment. This is particularly important for a new medical team that has no previous experience with your child.

A few years ago Kelsey had a bad reaction to anesthesia. After her surgery, she was having a hard time breathing and I saw that. She started to fight and hit, which people do when they can't breathe. But so many people including doctors assume that when someone has as significant a disability as Kelsey, that when they start hitting, they are being aggressive. And they want to stop it. I kept saying, "No, that's not it. She's having a hard time breathing. That's why she's acting like this." They gave her medication to settle her down. She was already having a hard time breathing and she stopped breathing. She ended up on a respirator for three weeks. It made me see, one more time, that doctors need to listen to the parents. The doctor on call was not one of her regular doctors and he did not know Kelsey. One of her regular doctors said, "You should not have let them do anything until you had called me."

(Chylene, mom of Kelsey who
was born with CMTC Syndrome)

If your child has a fatal condition, doctors may not be able to predict accurately how long your child will survive or what your child will be able to do.

A big part of his brain was missing. But Joey did the impossible. They told me that he could not see but he would follow me with his eyes. He would touch your very soul with his glances. At night before I would go to bed, I would go in to Joey and tell him, "Night Night." He would go, "Ugh!" for me to hold him. This was every night. The nurse would put a duck on the corner of his blanket and he would reach out and knock that duck off. He was an absolute miracle.

(Erin, mom of Joey who
was born with Trisomy 18)

Society, including the medical community, has mixed attitudes toward disability. Prepare to advocate for your child. You may feel like you are the only one who values her life.

The teaching hospital is equipped for special needs access. "We care about the person with special needs and so we have this special ramp, this ramp you can use to wheel your pregnant carcass up on your way to abort your twenty-week-old Down syndrome baby per the good doctor's suggestion." [*The prejudice against children with Down syndrome*] didn't end with doctors. We talked to others who said that when their children were born, instead of sending flowers, people sent apologies. One person told me some particularly cruel comments another mother made at a playground. Another said her doctor was disgusted that she wouldn't abort her child. Yeah, our culture really "cares" about those with special needs. Is it any wonder moms get the impression that Down syndrome (or anything else) is hopeless and cave under the pressure and fear?

(Ashli, mom of Emmil who was born without Down syndrome)

You may be offered nontreatment for a possibly correctable problem.

Karen's heart defect was not quite as bad as originally thought and could be corrected with one open-heart surgery. I was shocked when the cardiologist told me he would support me 100 percent if I decided not to agree to the surgery and allow her to die. This was especially hard to hear because, as a nurse, I knew that the doctor would have been otherwise enthusiastic about an operation offering a 90 percent chance of success — if my child didn't also have Down syndrome.

(Nancy, mom of Karen who was born with Down syndrome)

You may have to fight for your child's treatment.

The neurosurgeon decided the shunt was not working and that she needed a different one. Just days before Thanksgiving, they did the surgery. We were in the hospital for three very long months. We literally had to fight for Karlee's life 24/7. We never left the hospital. Finally, in February, we returned home.

(Katie, mom of Karlee Rose, Benal, and Nikki, all of whom were born with spina bifida)

No one can predict with complete accuracy what your child can achieve. Strive to have your child reach his potential by giving your child every opportunity at a normal and full life.

I learned to walk with a prosthesis at the age of fifteen months, and I have been walking, running and playing sports ever since. I have participated in track-and-field and figure skating. I've played volleyball with our school team, I've taken swimming lessons for over five years, completing eight levels and I played softball in high school girls' league.

(Stacy, an adult who was born with disfigurement of her left hand and an above knee amputation due to amniotic band syndrome)

[T]he doctors had told her that Charity would be unable to enjoy any of her senses. She wouldn't be able to see, hear, feel, taste, or smell. She would know nothing of what was going on around her, would never have any control over any part of her body, would never experience or be able to express joy, happiness, and love....[8] What

---

8. Blaine M. Yorgason, *One Tattered Angel* (Draper, Utah: Gentle Breeze Publications, 1995), 43.

was most amazing to me, though, was her personality. She loved to be held and cuddled, she fussed if she didn't get her bottle on time, she enjoyed taking baths, and more and more her radiant smile was becoming a sought-after reward by all of us....[9] Not only could she hear, she could obviously hear well! No matter how quiet we tried to be, she could always tell when one of us was near. And she visibly reacted to external sounds. For instance, she loved music (the real kind, rather than my singing), but only certain types.[10]

(Blaine, adoptive father of Charity who
was born with severe brain loss)

Sometimes parents have low expectations of what their child can achieve. Fight these thoughts and let your child try. Expect your child to do as much for himself as possible.

When she got to be about two years old, I was thinking about how most two-year-olds walk around in their parents' shoes and how Jessica would never do that because of her limb differences. The next thing I know she puts the shoes on her arms and comes clomping into the kitchen in them.

(Patricia, mom of Jessica who was born
with limb differences of both arms and both legs)

Dealing with Professionals

YOU are the expert on YOUR child. Doctors study symptoms and diseases. YOU study YOUR child. YOU know when something does not seem right. If a doctor minimizes symptoms that alarm you, get a second opinion. And maybe a third. If suggested treatment seems wrong to you, make the specialist justify it.

When Kelsey was three years old, she was really, really sick. We made a decision that we wanted to bring her home, to be held and be with the family. We felt she spent way too much time in the hospital. So we got an oxygen tent and we got suctioning and nurses and we brought everything home with us. Some doctors told us that we were in denial and we didn't understand what we were doing and this wasn't the best for Kelsey, but we just felt that she needed love and she needed to be out of the hospital. She got better. When she was a baby, I saw this spark in her eyes that she was a fighter and I felt like she was starting to lose it. She got that spark back in her eyes again. Not that she hasn't been back in the hospital and not that she hasn't gone through difficult times because she has, but she hasn't lost that spark again.

(Chylene, mom of Kelsey who
was born with CMTC Syndrome)

---

9.   Ibid., 63.

10. Ibid.

Depending on the advice given, ask yourself if you believe that:

ॐ Your child will outgrow the concern.

ॐ You might be hostile, overprotective, or causing the problem.

ॐ This problem really ought to be left untreated.

ॐ The treatment suggested makes sense.

ॐ Continuing treatment that is not working now is magically going to work.

ॐ Your child ought to be denied the treatment protocol because he is not "normal" so "what good will it do?"

ॐ Your child will never _____ (fill in the blank).

I have a ten-year-old son who was born at twenty-six weeks. He had a very difficult NICU stay with the worst complication being lung hemorrhage and cardiac arrest that lasted thirty minutes when he was twenty days old. The NICU doctors advised us not to continue with any heroic measures since it could only result in severe multiple disabilities. It would be the best and kindest thing to let him die. His life would be nonproductive and full of pain. Alex will never be "normal" but he surely has had a fulfilling life and has made an impact on just about everyone he meets. The brain is a strange and wondrous organ, and x-rays and scans can't predict outcomes. Alex had a CAT scan. He has "catastrophic" loss of white matter; the gray matter is encroaching where the white matter should have been. At ten, he talks (nonstop, it seems at times) clearly and understandably and has a very extensive vocabulary. He is in a regular third grade classroom with needed supports. He is below grade level in many areas, but his personality makes him just one of the kids. He plays ball with the Miracle League of Michigan. When Alex was about five or six and just becoming aware that he was the only one in the school with a wheelchair and thick glasses, I was getting him ready to catch the lift bus to school and he looked me in the eye and asked why he couldn't walk like everyone else. So, as I buckled the straps on his wheelchair, I told him he was born too early and too small (smaller than a two pound can of tomatoes) and that his heart had stopped and it caused a big boo-boo in his brain. That the doctors told us that the boo-boo would make it so he couldn't walk and that he couldn't eat, think or talk ("They said I wouldn't be able to talk Mom????"). He thought a minute, looked at me and said, "Know what Mom? I sure fooled all those doctors."

(Joanne, mom of Alex who
was born with multiple disabilities)

Select a professional who:

- ❧ Takes time with your child.
- ❧ Knows how to speak to and handle your child to minimize anxiety.
- ❧ Answers questions in understandable terms.
- ❧ Listens to you.
- ❧ Respects your judgment.
- ❧ Welcomes your opinion and suggestions.
- ❧ Treats you as part of the team.
- ❧ Is humble enough to say, "I do not know, but I will try to find out."
- ❧ Will suggest a specialist or second opinion.
- ❧ Has a positive outlook and will help your child reach her potential.
- ❧ Clearly outlines goals and time frames.

Help any professional with whom you work to display such qualities by asking questions such as these:

- ❧ Would you please explain that again?
- ❧ May I share my experience with my child in this regard?
- ❧ What is the low and high spectrum of what children like mine can achieve? What is the source of this information so that I may research it myself?
- ❧ What goals do you see for my child? What is your projected time frame in meeting them?
- ❧ What is your plan if goals are not met on time?

Evaluate decisions as they are made and results as they are seen (or not seen). If a decision does not lead to the expected result, reevaluate and decide anew. Fight the tendency to look back and regret a choice. You made the best choice you could with the information you had. You may have new or more information now, but you did not have it then. Regretting past choices is a bottomless pit. Avoid it.

To prepare for visits with professionals:

- ❧ Read up on your child's condition and on what children with it can and cannot do. Be prepared to present this to the experts.
- ❧ Talk to other parents about their children's achievements.
- ❧ Make a list of your questions and concerns.
- ❧ If you have a particular concern, keep a log of your child's behavior and bring it with you to document your sharing.
- ❧ Get to the topic at hand and stick to it.
- ❧ If you dislike what you are hearing, politely but firmly speak up.
- ❧ Ask questions if you do not understand something.
- ❧ Say no to things that make you uneasy.

〜 Form a partnership with the professionals.

〜 Ask if you may tape-record the conference, then review it later.

〜 Take notes.

Keep dated records of all medications, treatments, options, therapies, phone numbers, ID numbers, phone and office consultations, and evaluation and assessment reports. File all these in chronological order. You will be able to compare current and previous information quickly and easily.

If you feel that a professional is not acting properly, find one who will treat your child better.

> Early intervention taught me to advocate and gave me the confidence I needed to stand up to the docs. I asked questions and got answers. Just because Alex had brain damage wasn't a reason they couldn't do something to help. My biggest obstacle was being "nice and polite." The first time I fired a specialist, it was the respiratory doc. He ordered another pH probe after the fundo/g-tube had been placed. Alex began to get ill and developed a fever and his breathing was beginning to sound a bit weird, just the beginning of something and mom's instinct. The doc blew off my concerns, said Alex was fine and did another pat on the head thingie. I had started to butt heads with this doc about two or three months earlier when I refused to give Alex a medicine he prescribed. Alex developed a rash and his pediatrician determined it was an allergic reaction to the med. The respiratory doc said no one was allergic to the med and to continue giving it to Alex, and I refused. Just the same, when I fired him I was actually worried about hurting his feelings, and my knees were shaking. It wasn't something that was easy to do but, believe me, it was liberating. The couple of times I ran into a doc that didn't believe in Alex as a viable human being, it got so much easier [*to speak up*]. I learned to take steps to bring the doctor's behavior and attitude to the attention of those in authority, the head of the department, insurance companies, patient relations. Now I don't even quiver a little.
>
> *(Joanne, mom of Alex who*
> *has multiple disabilities)*

Summary of How to Live

Kathie Snow, in her book *Disability Is Natural*, summarizes the following points for success:

〜 Do not worry.

〜 Focus on your child, not the disability.

〜 Have your child in as natural an environment as possible.

〜 Presume that your child is competent.

〜 Have high expectations.

ॐ Meet your child's unique needs.

ॐ Provide tools for success.

ॐ Help your child naturally.

ॐ Experience the dignity of risk.

ॐ Anticipate criticism.

ॐ Protect your child's privacy.

ॐ Listen to your inner voice.[11]

The Ten Commandments for Parents[12] *of Handicapped Children*

1. Take one day at a time, and take that day positively. You don't have control over the future, but you do have control over today
2. Never underestimate your child's potential. Allow him, encourage him, expect him to develop to the best of his abilities.
3. Find and allow positive mentors: parents and professionals who can share with you their experience, advice, and support.
4. Provide and be involved with the most appropriate educational and learning environments for your child from infancy on.
5. Keep in mind the feelings and needs of your spouse and your other children. Remind them that this child does not get more of your love just because he gets more of your time.
6. Answer only to your conscience: then you'll be able to answer to your child. You need not justify your actions to your friends or the public.
7. Be honest with your feelings. You can't be a super-parent twenty-four-hours a day. Allow yourself jealousy, anger, pity, frustration, and depression in small amounts whenever necessary.
8. Be kind to yourself. Don't focus continually on what needs to be done. Remember to look at what you have accomplished.
9. Stop and smell the roses. Take advantage of the fact that you have gained a special appreciation for the little miracles in life that others take for granted.
10. Keep and use a sense of humor. Cracking up with laughter can keep you from cracking up from stress.[13]

---

11.   Snow, 436–440.

12.   People First Language would read "Children with Disabilities."

13.   Reprinted with permission from Spina Bifida Family Support and reprinted from a posting to the Children's Special Health Care Needs Mailing List, [CSHN-L] sponsored by the University of Florida's Institute for Child Study. http://www.tacanow.com/commandments.htm.

8

INTO THE FUTURE WITH A CHILD WHO SURVIVES

We cannot do everything, and there is a sense of liberation in realizing that. This enables us to do something, and to do it very well.

Oscar Romero[1]

What You've Taught Me

Ah, Kay-Marie, what have you taught me?
That our expectations are not always met,
That our fantasies are indeed fantastic,
For reality is far richer than anything we can imagine.
You have taught me
That artificial limbs are much less trouble
Than PMS in a teenager,
That a mind that struggles with math
Might soar when it comes to oils, acrylics, and pottery,
That it is better to never be able to ballet
Than it is to never be able to live.
You've taught me that the worst I thought of you
Never materialized
And the best I thought
You far surpassed.
Back when we adopted you
I could not know the future.
But if I had known it,
I'd take it all again —
The trials and the triumphs —
Because they mean you are in our lives.

*Madeline Pecora Nugent, mom of Kay-Marie
who was born with two lower limb differences*

Being a Normal Family

How you deal with your child, and how you allow society to deal with him, will determine whether or not you are a "normal" family. Carry on with whatever activities are normal for your family, making the necessary adjustments to include your child.

---

1.   http://www.epica.org/Library/editors/editors-14.htm.

As the weeks went on, her seizures and apnea increased. We got used to it. We took her to Grandma's, the mall, the park and we took several walks around the block. We tried to make it as normal as we could. Hospice was a tremendous support. The nurse was on call 24/7. She would come as often as I wanted. In addition, we had a nun, a dietician and a social worker supporting us throughout our time with Grace. We wanted things to be as normal as possible.

(Christine, mom of Grace Ann
who was born with Trisomy 18)

All children, not just those with differences, require time, input, and concern.

It is a little crazy with all the doctors' appointments. Sometimes, I feel frustrated because I don't know what is wrong. Emily has taught me to appreciate the little things in life, not to take anything for granted, especially love and health. I love the cuddles, the smiles and giggles, and just giving her a bath. Story time is so special with the three youngest. Even though my sixteen-year-old is driving me crazy, I look at her and realize one day she is going to be out on her own, living her own life, and I pray I have taught her right from wrong, how to protect herself, manage money, and how to love unconditionally. It takes a lot out of you emotionally when you have children, not just ones with special needs.

(Sabra, mom of Emily who was
born with enlarged ventricles in her brain)

"But," you object, "normal children do not require this level of attention."

Not so. All infants and toddlers need a great deal of attention.

"But those children will grow out of needing that much care. My child never will."

That may be true, but why should that fact keep your family from being "normal"?

Kelsey has been part of all our family vacations. She uses a sit ski to ski with us. She loves roller coasters, speedboats, anything fast. One of our nurses put in for us for a Wish Come True (Kelsey had been very sick) so we went to Disney World. Kelsey goes into the water in her beach chair. We have a family Easter egg hunt every year. Kelsey is in Girl Scouts. She's been on a whale watch, went to New York on the train, and went to Discovery Cove and swam with dolphins. In school, with support, she walked across the stage for her eighth grade graduation. She brought attendance down every morning to the school office. She's been in Special Olympics and got some awards. She can bowl. We can push her chair right next to the ramp — we put the ball there and Kelsey pushes the ball down. She's out on the court playing basketball with her friends. Eight kids came over and we had a birthday party. Just meeting Kelsey for the first time you don't realize how much she enjoys life.

(Chylene, mom of Kelsey who
was born with CMTC Syndrome)

We decided that we needed to keep our lives as normal as possible. We needed to have fun, "make memories," and try to be a normal family. So we took Nathan everywhere we went unless he was not well. All our friends loved him and felt very comfortable with him. He was recognized and known to the people at stores we frequented. The more normally we treated him, we figured, the more normally people would see him. We traveled, camped (in my folks' motor home, so we had electricity for Nathan's feeding pump), went out to dinner, to church, concerts, movies and school activities, etc. We had a very good life together.

(Jennifer, mom of Nathan who
was born with Menke's Disease)

What are "normal" families like? Normal families:

- Love one another.
- Do things together.
- Help one another.
- Disagree sometimes but love each other anyway.
- Endure sibling rivalry.
- Support each other.

Our pediatrician team told us about occupational therapy, and friends referred us to a prosthetic company. Marissa has had six prostheses for her absent left hand. She's a ballerina and plays violin. She is super smart, a talented singer, and does not let her disability hold her down. In fact, she does not view her absent left hand as a disability as she's had it all her life. Right now Marissa is very involved in musical theater.

(Mary, mom of Marissa who was born
without a left hand due to amniotic band syndrome)

Being a normal family requires some risks. Every child takes risks. Think of toddlers learning to climb stairs or older children climbing trees or learning to ride horses. The potential for injury may be present, but does that mean your child should not try?

Kelsey has a few seizures a week. We have to be careful because we like her to be as independent as possible. We like her to use her walker and to sit in chairs other than her wheelchair, but we have to be really careful and watch for signs of a seizure. Once she was sitting at the kitchen table — she doesn't use her wheelchair at the table — but I just turned her away from the table and she had a seizure, fell forward, and broke her two front teeth. They got bonded. They didn't fall all the way out.

(Chylene, mom of Kelsey who
was born with CMTC Syndrome)

As you learn day by day, you will find that you are dealing successfully with your child's differences. Life assumes a manageable routine, and joy returns.

Vikki grew beautifully. With physical therapy and all the other therapies, she crawled at thirteen months and walked at nineteen months. To think that they gave her a thirty percent chance of ever walking! My son Michael is now sixteen and he is hanging in there at school (eleventh grade). He continues to struggle with his ADD stuff and just being a teen. He has had no problems with his left foot/leg, other than dealing with its limitations and lack of muscle in the calf. He's ALWAYS a challenge! But I love him so! Victoria will soon be twelve. She is beautiful! We haven't had any major surgeries or hospitalizations since she was a year old. She hasn't been on medication for about two years and has stayed relatively healthy. She did develop an increased scoliosis (twenty-six degrees). She will be wearing a body jacket for at least eighteen months. She wears arch inserts in her shoes and a night brace on her left big toe that has developed crooked. She is simply amazing and really a happy kid! We are EXTREMELY close and love to sing in the church choir together. She is also on the honor roll and citizenship at school. She is my hero!!

(Susan, mom of Victoria Ann who was born
with spina bifida and of Michael who was born with a club leg)

Marriage

Parenting a child with differences necessitates new decisions, adjustments, and attitudes. Marriages may break up when a spouse cannot adjust, gives undue attention to the needier child, or refuses to help in child care. Many of these marriages would have dissolved over another issue at a later time, because every marriage is, at some time, subject to unexpected stresses and changes.

Avoid the pitfalls by:

- Communicating with one another.
- Refusing to blame.
- Integrating your child into your life instead of having your life revolve around your child.

➣ Trying to understand your spouse's emotions.

➣ Helping out.

➣ Discussing treatments and therapies together.

➣ Jointly attending sessions with professionals.

➣ Sharing child care.

➣ Compromising.

➣ Creating an emergency procedure — who does what.

➣ Selecting which parent will have the final say if you cannot agree.

Financial Concerns

Finances might be a concern.

> Finances were the biggest difficulty we had. We had insurance, but it didn't cover everything, and there were big deductibles each year. We qualified for skilled nursing care, but the expense was so great that we seldom used it unless absolutely necessary. We eventually took out a mortgage to pay medical bills. We felt like we were always living on the edge financially. We'd made a decision that I would stay home with our children, and, when Nathan was diagnosed, it became a necessity. Our one income was stretched way too tightly. Our medical expenses were so high that they ate up anything we might otherwise have saved. And because we had a middle-class income, we fell through the cracks when it came to getting any assistance.
>
> *(Jennifer, mom of Nathan who*
> *was born with Menke's Disease)*

Insurance may pay for your child's medical bills. If you are refused assistance, be sure that the refusal is lawful. Parents have been told that they were ineligible for medical insurance when such was not the case. Double check with other agencies and officials.

If insurance does not pay all your bills, contact local charitable, church, and governmental agencies that can help. Support groups can also provide guidance. Keep searching until you discover all the help for which your child may qualify.

Friends and family, veterans, church and civic groups may begin a non-profit fund for your child's medical needs. Many people and organizations are willing to assist. Fund-raisers are limited only by the imagination. Be sure to write a thank-you note to every group that helps.

If you need more financial help, turn to your local congressperson. In the United States, this would be your state or national representative. Involve your senators, too. Also call local television and radio stations and local newspapers about your dilemma. The more publicity, the better the chance of obtaining funds.

The Internal Revenue Service or other tax offices can help you determine whether your purchases are tax-deductible.

Some employers can make adjustments for parents of children who need special care.

> My boss said, "Why not work at home for the rest of your pregnancy?" and, after Mikey was born, he said, "Why not continue working at home?" I work from home and have a nanny to take care of Mikey. I can hear him constantly. When I want to take a break from work, I go and play with Mikey for a few minutes.
>
> *(Jennifer, mom of Mikey who*
> *was born with cloacal exstrophy)*

Sometimes a change of attitude makes a big difference.

> One day I was talking with a friend at church. He and his wife had multiple miscarriages and then finally gave birth to three children, each more premature than the one before. All lived but had very rocky beginnings. I asked him how they dealt with the stress of all the medical bills. He said, "Well, some people have car payments and house payments. We have kid payments." A load slid from my shoulders at that moment. I would do or pay ANYTHING to help Nathan to live and to have a good life. Suddenly I had a new perspective. I won't say the financial stress wasn't still there, but now we could look at the bills as something we were doing for our child, and not as a purely negative thing.
>
> *(Jennifer, mom of Nathan who*
> *was born with Menke's Disease)*

Teasing

As your child grows up, other children may tease or ridicule him for being different.

> I am born with deformed fingers. Everything was great till I started school. Then the teasing started. Almost every day they teased me 'cause of my fingers. I was scared to walk home from school alone and had almost no friends in school. Teachers just said, "Don't care about them. Then they will stop." They didn't stop. One day my mom was outside hanging up clothes and I came home from school. I walked just past her and asked out of the blue, "What is the reason for me to live?" I didn't try to kill myself but I had that thought lots of times.
>
> *(Elin, a young woman with neurofibromatosis,*
> *as well as digit loss due to amniotic band syndrome)*

Everyone in my town and school knows who I am and the reason behind my disability. Everyone understands, and they have learned to look past it to see the real me. When I was seven years old, my family moved. This was a shocking experience. No one knew who I was, and they didn't understand me. It was hard to make new friends, and I was constantly stared at. After a few months, we moved back home to the people who understood me.

(Stacy, an adult who was born with disfigurement of her left hand and an above the knee amputation due to amniotic band syndrome)

As a parent, you may be more aware of staring or negative responses than your child is.

Just the other day in the store, a man, his wife, and their six children were staring at Jessica, and they were not ten feet away from us. They were speaking Spanish, which I do not speak, so I felt they would not understand anything I said to them. I wanted to say something mean. Then we left the store, and one of my older daughters asked Jessica if she had noticed the staring. She said no. She had been looking at other things.

(Patricia, mom of Jessica who was born with limb differences of both arms and both legs)

While you cannot fight your child's battles, you can educate his school peers by talking to them about congenital disabilities and helping them to understand your child. This takes the mystery out of the disability and may make your unique child one of the most popular.

There were kids whose parents requested that their kids be in Kelsey's class because those kids would learn to be more compassionate and caring.

(Chylene, mom of Kelsey who was born with CMTC Syndrome)

When your child is able, teach him to speak up for himself.

I told Jessica, "When people stare, just wave or say Hi!"

(Patricia, mom of Jessica who was born with limb differences of both arms and both legs)

When I was nineteen was the last time anyone teased me. That boy was about two years younger than me He asked me where I was hiding my fingers. I asked him where he had hidden his brain.

(Elin, a young woman with neurofibromatosis, as well as digit loss due to amniotic band syndrome)

Children often view themselves differently than they will when they are older.

Kay-Marie was born with two lower limb differences and other difficulties. Today she runs her own floral design business.

I was at the store to buy some candy when I was twelve years old. A lady asked me, "Did you lose your fingers in a meat cutter?" I said, "No, I was born like this." That lady should have known better than asking that to a twelve-year-old kid. Now sometimes, when I am on the bus or the subway, people ask me, "Can I ask you a personal question?" I say, "Yes. Sure." I know what they will ask. And then they ask me what happened. I tell them and they say, "Oh, OK!" I think it is OK that they ask rather than think I lost my fingers. We have students in our daycare who at times ask me what happened, and I say I was born like this. Sometimes no one notices it before I tell them.

(Elin, a young woman with neurofibromatosis,
as well as digit loss due to amniotic band syndrome)

I have found ways to deal with people staring. I simply smile. If a young child has questions about my appearance, I feel honored to answer and give them a better understanding.

(Stacy, an adult who was born with amniotic band syndrome which
caused disfigurement of her left hand and an above the knee amputation)

Instill pride and self-worth in your child, and you may be surprised to see how your grown child views what you may have considered a tragedy.

I am a member of The War Amps Champ Program. I regularly attend their seminars to learn about new technology for amputees. They have helped me understand who I am and that I should be proud of what I have accomplished.

(Stacy, an adult who was born with amniotic band syndrome which
caused disfigurement of her left hand and an above the knee amputation)

My fingers were completely webbed at birth, and both hands were joined. The plastic surgeon has done an amazing job. I did have a few problems at school, mainly other kids picking on me because none of us had ever seen anything like it! My mum told me I was special, but it does little to ease the pain when you're six and struggling to fit in. But now I don't even really think about it. It's only when I notice someone looking at me sideways, that I remember, "Oh yeah, I'm special." As soon as I got over trying to hide it, life became a lot easier. My one regret is that living in a jandal [*thong, flip-flop*] nation I don't have the toes to hold them on!!

(Kirsty who was born with deformities of
the hands and feet due to amniotic band syndrome)

Make a Way

If you want your child to be included in a certain class or program and are meeting resistance from those in charge, talk to the officials. Educating them about your child's abilities and needs may be enough to grant your child access to the group.

Our church, St. Lucy's, has learned from Kelsey. They were nervous when I went to sign up Kelsey for CCD [*Confraternity of Christian Doctrine, a program of religious instruction in Roman Catholic parishes*]. They first said, "Do you mean we'll get a special class for Kelsey?" I said, "No, that's not what I was thinking. I was thinking that Kelsey would be with the kids her age just like anyone else would. Obviously I'd go with her or teach the class." It took some work for St. Lucy's to help Kelsey figure it out.

(Chylene, mom of Kelsey who
was born with CMTC Syndrome)

The group may be concerned about your child's medical needs. They may feel that they are not equipped to handle an emergency. Have a plan worked out for emergencies *before* you talk to any group. This way you will answer an objection before it is raised.

If you want an experience for your child that is unavailable in your community, you could begin something new.

I started a summer camp for Kelsey. We have a lot of fun. The camp is six weeks. It is exhausting, but I love it. We have about thirty staff and have sixty-five kids that attend. It's not just for kids with disabilities. Parents hear about it and want their kids to be included. I have the support of family and Looking Upward — when I went to them and told them about the summer camp, they were supportive.

(Chylene, mom of Kelsey who
was born with CMTC Syndrome)

Understanding Developmental Stages

All children progress through the same developmental stages. A cognitive disability can slow down the stages or may cause development to end at one stage. A child may skip a stage. Recognizing the stages will help you understand what is appropriate for that stage. Books, articles, websites on child development, and other parents can provide in-depth insights.

In brief, some of these stages are:

1. Child is focused totally on self and his or her own needs.

2. Child learns what behaviors work to get needs met and uses those behaviors.

3. Child begins to see things from another's viewpoint but still sees self as most important.

4. Child begins to make judgments about what is normal and usual based on his or her own experience. Things that are not normal or usual in this child's experience seem "bad" or "wrong."

5. Child develops limited empathy for others, including inklings that experiences other than his or hers may be "normal" to others.

6. Child begins to notice and dislike differences between self and others. Child wants to fit in.

7. Child begins to see parents as repressive, controlling, outdated, unsympathetic, and stupid, and turns to peers for understanding and support.

8. Child begins to realize that parents are not as incompetent and that peers are not as smart as previously imagined. Relationship with parents becomes more of a mentor/friend relationship than an antagonistic one.

Generally stages 1–4 occur during infancy and young childhood. Stages 5–6 develop in preadolescence, stage 7 occurs during adolescence and teen years, and stage 8 in young adulthood.

Whose Dreams?

"My mother listened to me and then quietly said, 'I know that thinking about all of those things is very painful right now, but you have to remember that those are your dreams, sweetheart, not hers. Jesse will have dreams of her own. They may not be like those of other children, but they will be her dreams just the same.' "[2]

---

2. Ann Waldrop, "Dreams," in *You Will Dream New Dreams*, 113.

Talk with your child about his dreams. Brainstorm together ways to make them come true. Persevere in making them happen.

> My son Jonny, now twelve, is a snappy dresser and an avid movie/
> Broadway buff, with a repertoire including songs from *Phantom of
> the Opera, Annie, Bye Bye Birdie,* and more. He loves people of all
> ages, but babies make him turn to mush. He has an uncanny way
> with animals. He loves school, but that doesn't keep him from loving
> the thrill of snow days more.
>
> *(Barbara, mom of Jonathan, Jesse, Daniel, and Justin,
> all of whom were born with Down syndrome)*

Your child will realize her dreams if you help. Build your child's self-esteem and self-confidence. Only by helping your child be as independent as possible, as early as possible, will you prepare her for adulthood.

> It's all how you treat it. She does not hide her hand from kids
> who walk up and ask what happened. When kids say, "Where's your
> hand?" and ask her what happened, she says, "That's the way God
> made me." Now she is almost three. She puts her socks on, her shoes,
> pants, and shirt, combs her hair, holds crayons, and paper. She does
> not like us to touch her hand or give it too much attention, but when
> it's time for her to roughhouse and play with you she will reach out
> and will wave with her little hand.
>
> *(Annalee, mom of Brooke who was born
> with nodules for fingers and a boneless thumb on her left hand)*

Here are some suggestions to help your child realize her dreams:

- Praise your child for jobs well done and efforts sincerely made, even if they are not totally successful.

- Create situations that will build your child's self-confidence and self-worth. Capitalize on your child's talents.

- Even though you could do something more quickly, allow your child to do it so he learns his capabilities. Sometimes this means watching your child struggle even though you want to help.

- Avoid the pity pot. Pitying your child will not help. Respect your child and use his or her strengths for encouragement.

- Do not baby or allow your youngster to get away with behavior you would not tolerate in other children.

- Ask your child's input on decisions that involve him or her. Implement your child's ideas as much as possible.

- Overestimate rather than underestimate what your child can do.

If you raise the bar, your child may reach it. Try and see without frustrating your child.

❧ Teach your child personal care skills. This may mean allowing some things to be done less perfectly than you can do them. It may also mean some adjustments such as short haircuts or using slip-on shirts and Velcro zippers.

❧ Give your child chores. Only expect as much perfection as your child can achieve.

❧ Within reason, adapt the house to the child, but remember that other family members live there also and that your child will have to live in a society that is not 100 percent suited to his needs.

❧ Integrate your child into society. Help him or her to deal with questions and responses. Teach how to interact politely with adults, to make purchases, order from menus, and negotiate streets as much as possible. Teach your child as many social survival skills as can be learned. These are skills adults need.

❧ Encourage your child to make friends. You may have to bring your child to other children or bring them to your child. Teach your child the skills needed to be a good friend.

❧ Help your child to understand and accept personal differences as the source of abilities and insights other youngsters do not have. Help your child share his or her talents with others.

❧ Encourage hobbies and special interests so that your child uses leisure time wisely. These could become hallmarks of recognition and sometimes of income.

❧ Incorporate some structure into your life. Schedules work well, even if you cannot always meet them, because they keep you focused and help your child anticipate what is coming next.

❧ Think radical new thoughts. Society has set certain educational goals for every child. Maybe your child can meet them. Maybe not. Brainstorm ways to develop your child's skills. If society expected everyone to be auto mechanics, many people would be failures.

❧ Allow your child to make choices and then take responsibility for them. If the choice was good, the child will obtain the rewards. If poor, the child will suffer consequences which he needs to deal with himself. We mature by making decisions and then living with their results. Being self-determined is more important than any functional ability.

❧ Foster a sense of humor and perspective in your child.

❧ Do not allow others, including grandparents and other relatives, to pity, coddle, excuse, or belittle your child. Expect them to treat your child as you do. Reject any other behavior.

℞ Support your child's dreams. Instead of thinking and saying that your child could never achieve her fantasy, say and think, "If you really want to do that, we will look for a way to make it happen." Most outlandish dreams fade with time, but the reasonable ones persist. Your child will understand better than you do what is reasonable for her.

I see him working toward his dreams of becoming a veterinarian. He speaks of college, of a family of his own, of being on his own one day and not having his mom tell him to clean his room. Nick is a pretty average young man, with an above-average spirit.

(Ashley, mom of Nick who
was born with spina bifida)

Aim for full inclusion of your child into society. National disability organizations can refer you to laws that will help your child be part of the mainstream.

Schools

School can present problems. Teachers may not know how to deal with your child's needs. You may have to educate the teachers and other school personnel about how to treat your child.

Kelsey went to a school for children with disabilities until she was ready for kindergarten. Then she went to public school. She definitely paved the way for kids with very significant disabilities. When she first started school, she had to use oxygen and suction which made people nervous, but once they got over their fear, they were fine. Then there were field trips. I always say, "Kelsey should be treated just like any other child. If the kids in her class go on field trips, then Kelsey should go on field trips." They realized that Kelsey could be part of the class just like the other kids, and how much the other kids actually learned from her.

(Chylene, mom of Kelsey who
was born with CMTC Syndrome)

School personnel may assume that physical differences indicate mental disabilities. Teach them to think otherwise.

Before Jessica started school, she was scheduled for an IQ test. I asked, "Do they test every child before they start school?" "No," I was told, "only the ones whom they think will have learning disabilities." They tested Jessica, and she tested out much smarter than average.

(Patricia, mom of Jessica who was born
with limb differences of both arms and both legs)

In the United States, under federal special education law, children with disabilities are entitled to an IEP (Individual Education Plan). The IEP addresses the needs in specific terms with specific time frames. It should also tell who will provide what services to meet the needs. Parents are to help write the IEP and must approve it before it is implemented. Once you approve the initial IEP, you are allowing the school system to make provision for your child thereafter. You legally become one of a team, not the person who has the final say. If you disagree with this concept, think twice before approving an initial IEP.

Once your child has an IEP, under the law, you also must be invited to staff meetings. Take along an objective friend or relative so that you are not unnerved by the array of professionals. Listen. Be polite. Be assertive but not aggressive. Admit that the professionals have knowledge that you lack. Try to understand their perspective. But do not allow them to intimidate you. You are a professional, too! Nobody knows your child better than you do.

> Having a child with Down syndrome has helped me see there's infinitely more to life than intelligence, beauty and "perfection." It's also taught me that not everything can be measured in dollars and cents — the benefits of full inclusion extend beyond a child with Down syndrome to his classmates, teachers, family and friends.
>
> *(Barbara, mom of Jonathan, Jesse, Daniel, and Justin,*
> *all of whom were born with Down syndrome)*

Do not accept the authority of any "case manager" or "service coordinator" above your own. As a parent, you are the primary spokesperson and advocate for your child. You may have to fight to have the greatest say in how the school system treats a child. Therefore:

~ Advocate for what your child needs.

~ See that the learning environment is maximized for your child.

~ If you do not understand something, ask.

~ If you dislike something, say so.

~ If your child needs more services, request them.

~ If you question test results, ask for a retest or schedule an independent evaluation.

~ Be completely comfortable with the IEP before you sign your approval. Approval, however, does not mean that the IEP will be followed.

~ Follow up on the IEP and be sure that what is written is actually being done. If not, schedule a meeting with the school and discuss what changes need to happen. If you remain dissatisfied, take legal action. A lawyer can advise you.

When Kay-Marie entered high school, I homeschooled her in academic subjects while she took specials at the high school. I would meet with her high school team to go over her IEP (Individual Education Plan) and share with them what we were doing at home. The school saw me as part of Kay's educational team. I submitted to them a list of texts we used (some of them given us by the high school at our request), goals, and evaluation means at the beginning of the school year. At the end of the year, I gave the school samples of her work at home as well as her major exams and book reports.

(Madeline, mom of Kay-Marie who was
born with two lower limb differences)

Schools tend to look at children's limitations rather than skills. Talk to the school system to be sure they are giving your child the best.

At home or school or church, Jonny is the first to offer help, to comfort someone who's down, and to laugh uproariously at the punch lines. His preschool teacher named him Ambassador of Goodwill. His public school kindergarten teacher, after thirty-plus years of teaching, said she'd never seen children as loving and caring as Jonny's classmates. The secret, she said, was Jonny. In fact, I bet some people would rather spend a day with Jonathan than with the experts who comment on his right to exist.

(Barbara, mom of Jonathan, Jesse, Daniel, and Justin,
all of whom were born with Down syndrome)

If you have a solution to meeting your child's needs, share the solution with the school. If you do not have a solution, define the issue in this way: What would it take to _____ (the goal you want for your child)? Brainstorm solutions with school personnel.

Consider the school system a partner. Negotiate if necessary. If one school system is not cooperative, you may be able to enroll your child in another. Once a school begins to work with your child, they may find that gratitude has replaced their fears.

If Ben had not lived, his friends would not know him, the school's culture would be different and something less than it is now. Our community would be less bright and less humane. His sister's view of the world might have been more narrow. I would not know the people I know today. Ben enjoys his life, loves his family and appreciates every day. He wouldn't want to miss a single beat.

(Terry, mom of Ben who
was born with multiple disabilities)

Homeschooling

For some children and families, homeschooling is the best option. Lessons can be paced to meet the child's needs. Parents can spend more time on difficult subjects or can use alternate teaching methods. They can choose their child's friends from other homeschooling families, and generally those children are quite accepting of differences.

If you homeschool, cooperate with the local school system. Check with your state educational agency or other homeschooling parents to determine what your state laws require. Most school systems want a letter of intent to homeschool plus an outline of the year's curriculum, including texts, tests, and goals. Meet with school officials and share your plans. Be prepared for convincing arguments and promises aimed at having you change your mind, but be resolute. Let the school system know that you feel homeschooling is best for your child, but add that you will keep them informed of what you are doing. Then do it! Submit copies of major exams and reports to the school system. Each year request a meeting to update school officials on your child's progress. If you wish your child to reenter the school system in the future, your child's homeschooling achievements will be well documented, and the school will know that you are a cooperative and responsible parent.

When we adopted Kay-Marie, she was almost seven years old and still did not know all the letters of the alphabet. We enrolled her in public school kindergarten. However, with her entering puberty early and dealing with learning difficulties, Kay-Marie was forming the opinion that she was bad and stupid. Wishing to avoid a self-fulfilling prophecy, I did what I once swore I would never, ever do. Homeschool my kid. We began homeschooling in grade four, with an approved curriculum, a special education consultant provided by the curriculum company, and the full cooperation of the local school department. We linked up with two homeschooling parent groups so that Kay-Marie would have contact with her peers. When Kay entered ninth grade, we enrolled her in the public high school and worked with the guidance counselor, special education department, and school supervisor to create a curriculum in which Kay took specials at the high school but continued to be homeschooled in academic subjects. She did very well. Upon graduation four years later, she enrolled in and graduated from a professional six-month floral design school. She now has her own floral design business locally and on the web at www.littleflowerflorals.com

(Madeline, mom of Kay-Marie who was born with two lower limb differences)

Sibling Rivalry

Perfect families and perfect children do not exist. All parents get frustrated and in some way every child is difficult to raise. Accept your limitations and those of your spouse and children.

Every child finds something specifically objectionable about each brother and sister. If siblings do not complain about your child's differences, they will find something else to object to. Children may think that if their sibling had no disability, she would be the perfect playmate. This is a fantasy.

Most children think that siblings get more attention or better treatment than they do. Siblings are often jealous of one another and compete for parental attention. Your child with differences will compete, too. She may use her condition to gain favor or attention. Other children may invent or exaggerate their own "problems" to combat parental concern for the sibling.

You cannot eliminate sibling rivalry, but you can minimize it. Here are some tips:

- Prevent the child with a disability from becoming the focal point of the family.
- Try to spend as much time as possible with each child.
- Do things together as a family.
- Have a weekly "date" alone with each child.
- Find, foster, and praise each child's unique talents, especially in the presence of others.
- Treat the children equally. Punish and reward them equally.
- Give each child chores.
- Do not pamper your children.
- Avoid comparing one child with another.
- Establish rules and enforce them.
- Respect your children's desire to not always be attentive to the brother or sister with a disability.
- Do not make one child the slave of another.
- Encourage your children to participate in sports, clubs, artistic endeavors, and other recreational pursuits. Driving children to events can be tricky, but perhaps you can carpool or arrange for another parent to pick up your child.
- Begin a club in your home.
- Beware of trying to have another child compensate for the child with the disability.

Let your youngsters be themselves. Some siblings will spend a great deal of time ministering to their brother or sister, but thinking of these helpers as little saints is unfair. Allow them to express negative feelings and to relax their ministrations without feeling guilty. Other children will complain about nearly everything they "have to do" for their sibling. They may act out to get your attention. Resist labeling these children as "bad" or "selfish." Both saint and sinner are competing for parental love and affection. Every day determine how you can show that love and affection to all your children.

Encourage play between your children by praising them when they play well together. Use toys that lead to interaction. These include balls, blocks, puppets, bean bags, tinker toys, bowling, tea sets, costumes, plastic food, balloons, dolls, cars and trucks, marbles, and toy telephones. Activities that foster sibling interaction include acting out stories, playing ___ (school, house, policeman, fireman, dentist, rock star, fantasy figure, space hero, a type of animal, etc.), fixing simple snacks, singing, interactive sports (baseball, ping-pong, video games, fantasy games, cards, table games, dominoes, checkers, Frisbees), marching, tag, hide-and-seek, taking a walk.

> All his siblings loved Joey and treated him well. His two-year-old brother had a special bond with Joey and tried to make him smile and laugh by acting goofy. We used to put wigs on Joey and dress him up and enjoy him. He was in the family room and slept on the couch so he was in the middle of everything.
>
> *(Erin, mom of Joey who*
> *was born with Trisomy 18)*

Your attitude toward your child will influence how your other children view him. Being positive brings rewards.

> We are stronger spiritually, our children are more compassionate than their peers in general, and our family is stronger and more tightly knit than most families I know. Our kids are now twenty-one and twenty-six, and they have a compassion that is unusual, especially for their age. Of all their friends, they say ours is the healthiest family. I think having Nathan in our midst helped a lot, but I think we also probably handled it right because I know some other families have fallen apart when they had a child with disabilities born to them. Part of it is our faith — knowing that God loves us and that everything that has happened has been part of a greater plan. And part of it is probably my personality — I just tend to find the bright side to most things, and I've helped our kids to see things that way overall.
>
> *(Jennifer, mom of Nathan who*
> *was born with Menke's Disease)*

Beware of being overprotective. Overprotecting children can lead to lifelong helplessness and dependency, which can be a greater disability than the child's actual condition. Letting your six-year-old play alone in the backyard or your eight-year-old wait for the bus alone does not mean that you are neglectful or taking chances. It means you are allowing your child to mature and trusting her to make good decisions.

> When our twins were born, Marie was fine but Tina had no hip on one side and only a partial thigh on the other. Doctors told us that she would never be able to sit up by herself, so they made her a sitting prosthesis when she was three months old. After using it for three weeks, she was sitting up by herself. The doctors said that she would never be able to walk without crutches, but she learned to do that. Today Tina is married and working as a children's museum coordinator. She wears a bucket prosthesis and lives a very normal life. What a child can achieve is very much an individual case. It also depends on what the parents will allow the child to do. We had a five-year-old and a three-year-old son when Tina and Marie were born so it was difficult to be protective of one when we had the other three. Tina learned to take her lumps, and she did well because of it.
>
> *(Gloria, mom of Marie and of Tina who was born*
> *with lower limb congenital amputation)*

Sharing with Your Children

Let your children know that they can discuss anything with you, even their negative feelings. This is especially important for older children who may not want to upset you. Help your children understand that feelings are not right or wrong. They express emotion and ought to be recognized. If your children do not discuss feelings with you, they may seek out friends who may have much misinformation. Or they may never air their feelings, which in the long run is emotionally damaging.

If one child seems unconcerned about a differently abled sibling, do a little emotional "digging." Your compliant child may not want to worry you while inside may be fretting. Sometimes making up a story can open communication. One possible story, Hannah Bear's Baby Brother, appears in Appendix F.

Children often have many questions. What is wrong with my brother? Why did this happen? Is my sister in pain? Will this happen to me? Why does she act so strangely? Does my brother love us? Will he ever be able to _____? What am I supposed to do with my sister? Will she die? Be honest and truthful. Explain the situation in terms your children can understand. They can handle more than you realize.

You may be able to find some children's books on a particular disability. Read the books before sharing them with your children to be sure they represent the attitudes you want to foster.

How you respond to your children either promotes or hinders communication. Encourage communication by asking a question, not issuing a command or reprimand. Compare these different responses to the same comments.

> *Johnny:* I hate it when Jane moans like that.
> *Mom (response that shuts down communication):* What an awful way to feel! She cannot help it.
> *Mom (response that fosters communication):* I know it is troubling. Jane's moaning bothers me, too, even though she cannot help it. What do you think we can do to help her and us?
> *Sara:* I hate Billy.
> *Dad (response that shuts down communication):* What a terrible thing to say! He is your brother!
> *Dad (response that fosters communication):* I am glad you shared that, Sara. Why do say you hate Billy?
> *Marie:* You like Peter better than me.
> *Mom (response that shuts down communication):* I certainly do not. I love you both the same.
> *Mom (response that fosters communication):* What makes you think that I love Peter better than you, Marie?

Siblings often have good advice. Discussions with them may spark suggestions to make things more comfortable. Older siblings may want to be part of meetings with professionals or may wish to teach their brother or sister certain skills. Encourage these things.

Take care not to minimize another sibling's problems by comparing them to what your child with a disability can or cannot do. Every problem is important to the person experiencing it.

> *Justin:* Why do you always make peas, Mom? I hate them!
> *Mother (response that shuts down communication):* What are you complaining about? Laura would love to eat peas if she could.
> *Mother (response that fosters communication):* Everybody has foods they dislike, but it is good to try all kinds of foods. How about if I make corn tomorrow? You like that better than peas, I think.
> *Gracie:* Dad, I have to have those sneakers. Everybody has them. Pleeease. Everybody calls me a dork because I have to wear these dorky shoes.
> *Dad (response that shuts down communication):* Gracie, we are in the middle of a crisis with Sam! Why are you worried about a pair of sneakers when your brother cannot breathe right?

> *Dad (response that fosters communication):* Oh, Gracie.
> I want to talk to you about those sneakers. But your mom
> and I are trying to get Sam breathing right again and we
> have to do that first. How about if you go and find an ad
> with what you want and we can talk just as soon as we
> know Sam is OK?

You, as parents, will determine how your children view one another.
Love all your children. Value each one's unique qualities. Focus on
abilities. Raise your children to understand that everyone is equal and
everyone has issues. In time the difficulties shall pass.

If, despite your best efforts, one sibling has an especially difficult
time dealing with a brother's or sister's condition, consider professional
counseling. While the phone book can provide referrals, the best ones
generally come from other parents. Hospitals or places of worship may
be able to recommend local parent support groups or individual parents
to whom you can speak.

Before considering any sibling support group, realize that taking your
child to such a group implies that the child with differences is causing the
difficulty. This implication masks the reality that the issue runs deeper than
the disability. In order to find peace, the troubled child must uncover and
address the root issue. A professional counselor can assist with this.

Discipline

If you think a child is engaging in "attention-seeking" behavior, try to
determine if your intuition is correct. One easy way is to try to distract
the child from the complaint while providing her attention. Usually a
child will not be distracted from a legitimate complaint.

> Mother is in the midst of trying to feed four-year-old
> Jerald who cannot feed himself.
> *Amanda:* Oh, my stomach hurts, Mommy. Ooooh. I feel
> sick!
> *Mom:* I am sorry to hear that, Amanda. Oh, I just thought
> of something. You like brownies! How would you like to
> help me make some for dessert?

If Amanda is not feeling well, she is going to say she does not want
brownies; she wants her tummy to stop hurting. Mom ought to check
Amanda. If Amanda wanted to take mom's attention from Jerald,
Amanda will be excited about the brownies. Mom can instruct her to get
a bowl, pan, and spoon ready.

Christmas morning photo of Maddie with her four brothers, all of whom have Down syndrome. Left to right: Jonny, Daniel, Justin, and Jesse.

Your Children's Friends

Your child with a disability belongs in the community, with his or her brothers and sisters. Take your family on outings. Help your children understand that those who make fun of people with differences are to be educated and maybe even pitied.

Have friends over to play with your other children. Teach your children how to explain a sibling's disability to others who may ask. Use simple explanations such as, "Anna's body does not behave the same way yours does." Teach your child with differences to explain things herself. "God made me this way," is a good response to questions.

Friends should interact with all your children. Plan activities so that visitors can see that all children have fun, enjoy life, and have certain likes and dislikes.

During the first days of school, you and your child should cooperate with teachers to help educate fellow classmates. The teacher can prepare the class, your child, and you for this interaction. Have classmates interact with your youngster. Explain what she can and cannot do. Obtain beforehand the names of children who are most likely to bully or ridicule and have them do something positive with your child. Praise them for their efforts. The goal is to have schoolmates see your son or daughter as a person and to understand that bullying or making fun of him or her is something no one would ever want to do.

> As my son Matt said when Jonny was a just a toddler, "Wouldn't the world be a better place if everyone had a brother with Down syndrome?"
>
> *(Barbara, mom of Jonathan, Jesse, Daniel, and Justin,*
> *all of whom were born with Down syndrome)*

Your Child as an Adult

As your child matures, allow her to make more and more decisions. Teach him to be as independent as possible. Integrate your child into the world. Provide the training she needs to be successful. Have him do things for himself. Speak to lawyers and other professionals about trust funds, housing, social services, and financial aid. As with any child, you should appoint a guardian should you die unexpectedly. Draw up legal documents for the disposition of your estate as it relates to supporting your child. Share with your other children any long- and short-term plans. Siblings have a right to know how responsible they will be in the future for their brother or sister.

Some parents consider nursing care or group home care for their adult children. Their reasons are many. Some are:

- ❧ The adult child requires too much assistance to be able to live alone.
- ❧ The parents are getting too old.
- ❧ The child is getting too large.
- ❧ The child's needs are increasingly difficult to manage.
- ❧ Parents feel they are unable to parent their other children well.
- ❧ Parents want the child in a safe setting as parents face their own demise and deaths.

Be sure that the out-of-the-home care facility will meet your expectations. When can you visit? How will your son or daughter be spending his or her time? Is there an opportunity for employment? What care is offered? What are the safety precautions?

> It's been really hard to think about Kelsey getting older and getting a place of her own. At first, I thought, "I could never do that — let

someone else take care of her." But we have some other friends that also have children with disabilities, and we are looking at buying a house together and then the agency would help us to support the kids because we can't expect the state to take care of our kids forever. If we don't do something, then we may not have a lot of choice about where our kids live. We really want Kelsey to stay in this community because this is where people know her, where her friends are. If we get some families together to buy a house, then the state will help us to provide supports for our kids as they get older. The biggest expense for supporting our kids is hiring staff. Kelsey needs somebody around the clock. We have actually started a corporation. It's a little bit scary, but you have to do it.

(Chylene, mom of Kelsey who
was born with CMTC Syndrome)

When Christopher was about twelve, I began thinking about his future. The Sisters of Mercy operate a home for those with physical and mental differences. Christopher can be put on a waiting list and we would be just as proactive in his care if he were accepted into the home.

(Mary, mom of Christopher who
was born with multiple disabilities)

Children who have been in long-term foster care often continue in foster care as adults. This option provides stability and a family.

Sexuality

Your young adult may have sexual feelings and thoughts even if he cannot express them or would find it difficult to function sexually. Everyone has a need for affection and love, and these needs can mature as sexual attraction. Communicate with your child about her feelings. Explain pitfalls and sexual predators in terms your child can understand. Your young adult will have to learn to handle her own sexuality, but your instruction will provide the guidelines.

I'm twenty-nine now, have just had my first baby, who is perfect! I live life fairly normally, although typing is a little trickier for me than most!! I have a great family and a loving partner.

(Kirsty, who was born with differences of
the hands and feet due to amniotic band syndrome)

When your child enters the world of adulthood, he or she will be well prepared because of your efforts.

9

THE GIFT OF YOUR CHILD

For it is in giving that we receive.

Francis of Assisi[1]

Ready to Begin

Michelle and I were walking,
In amongst the trees, the birds, the animals
And the grasses swaying in the wind.

I felt you so close, Stephanie.
I've always felt you in nature,
But this time it was different.
I felt you intertwined with me.

I finally felt some of the peace
That I was told would come again.
For the FIRST time I could imagine
The next baby.
You weren't being forgotten,
I could feel you knew that.
I felt so close to you.

Michelle and I discussed bringing the next baby
To our favorite spot,
All cuddled in a baby sling.

That was last week.
My health has returned thanks to natural remedies.
I still feel that small amount of inner peace.
I still feel your presence very close to me.
I guess this means one thing, my sweet baby.
I am ready to begin.
Ready to begin the process of starting a new life.
Thank you, Stephanie, for staying by your Mummy's side.
You are helping me to begin again.
You, your big sister Michelle, and your Daddy.

Bernadette Zambri, May 17, 1993[2]

---

1. http://thinkexist.com/quotation/for_it_is_in_giving_that_we_receive/14808.html.

2. Reprinted with permission from *Morning Light: Miscarriage, Stillbirth, and Early Infant Death from a Catholic Perspective*, by Bernadette Zambri (Toronto, Ontario: Morning Light Ministry, c/o Saint Mary's Church, 11 Peter St. South, Mississauga Ontario, Canada L5H 2G1, 1998), 36.

Whether your child lives briefly or has a longer life, you, by giving birth to your child, will have given your child the gift of his or her life and of your love. Memories will surround these gifts.

Anniversaries

You will face many anniversaries. Anniversaries are times to write a letter to your child or to create a poem or memento, to plant a tree, or to make a visit to someone who might be lonely. Particularly if the anniversary is painful, allow yourself the full range of emotions but also work to bring good out of the pain. In this way, healing will come.

Gianna Christe Mariolina

Our baby Gianna was born
On December 29, 2003.
Our hearts were naturally torn,
When she died at p.m. 6:03.

But we knew when she closed her eyes,
She would open them up yet again;
To be happy forever in paradise,
Which has been hoped for by women and men.

On that night my family and I
Let our hearts and our tears be shed.
Our smiles were watery, few eyes were dry,
When we remembered the thought she was dead.

But not dead, do you see?
She is alive and awake.
She is happier than you and me.
But when I think of her my heart will still ache.

I know that my family has a private saint.
We can ask her to help us in troubles.
We can pray to her while we work, paint,
Rake, sing, and even when we're blowing bubbles.

> *Alayna Nagurny (age eleven) on the anniversary of*
> *her sister Gianna's death (December 29, 2004)*
> *(Gianna was born with Trisomy 13 and holoprosencephaly.)*

One anniversary will be the date of the prenatal test which revealed your child's condition. You may relive all the pain and confusion of that time. Look at the ultrasound photos and any other mementos you may have. If your child has died, visit his grave. If your child is alive, do something special with her. If your child is living elsewhere, visit if you can, or make a phone call to the adoptive parents or institution. Give a gift in your child's memory. Host a party or fund-raiser for those in need. Create positive memories for what you may have viewed as the worst day of your life.

Other anniversaries will be the date of your child's death, or dates of birth, surgery, or those associated with other parenting choices. Holidays will bring their own memories. Mother's and Father's Day can be especially difficult if your baby has died. Remember that you are always a parent and celebrate your special day.

Seemingly insignificant events may cause strong emotions to surface. Certain weather patterns, sights, sounds, smells, places, and even everyday chores can trigger memories. Embrace the emotions for as long as they last. Healing comes through these times.

You may feel pain over what might have been but was not. This does not mean that you are a bad parent who does not love your child. It means you are a normal parent who wants your child to have a perfect, happy, painless existence. All parents come to realize that this desire is an illusion. Whatever children we have, we move forward in love despite the imperfections and the pain.

Future Children

Parents often want additional children, but future pregnancies can be scary. You have many questions:

- ✎ If your child died, will a future pregnancy cause you to cherish that child less? Probably not.

> He was my pride and my joy, and he changed my life forever. He has deepened my faith, given me hope, and left me with such wonderful memories. Since then, I have had two more children, a boy and a girl, who are both in perfect health. But I will not ever forget my beautiful, precious Tanner.
>
> *(Renee, mom of Tanner who was born with posterior urethral valves)*

- ✎ Will you have another child with a disability?

> [W]hen I became pregnant with our third child, Matthew, I was seriously frightened. We had prenatal testing done. We didn't get the results until about three months before he was born. Not that we would have ever considered abortion, but we wanted to know so we would be prepared and could start treating right at birth if he was sick. He was born perfectly healthy, praise the Lord!
>
> *(Jennifer, mom of Nathan who was born with Menke's Disease)*

൙ Will having a "normal" child make you love the child with differences less?

൙ Is it fair to your child to want another?

> Our children were really young. I didn't tell them that the baby was going to die, and, when Andrew did, they were really sad. I got pregnant quickly after that and my children were very concerned and came for the birth of the next baby. Andrew's life and death are part of the life cycle, maybe not a usual part, but it happens.
>
> *(Emily, mom of Andrew who*
> *was born with Trisomy 13)*

൙ Will you have time to care for your child with a disability if you have another baby?

> In June, Celine became a big sister to Genevieve. Having a "baby" to focus on has helped our family to move beyond Celine's heart defects.
>
> *(Monica, mom of Celine who was born with*
> *hypoplastic right heart syndrome)*

You might find yourself mixing up your children's names, perhaps even calling a living child by the name of one who died. This is a positive sign that you remember and love all your children and also that you are a typical parent.

Try to relax and enjoy all your children. Your subsequent baby, born without a disability, is not going to be the "perfect" child. You may actually find it easier to raise the child with differences!

Some parents expand their families through the adoption of children with disabilities.

> When Karlee, who was born with spina bifida, was two, her baby brother Alec was born. He's a very normal, typical kid — no birth defects. Karlee loved little Alec. Then, in June of 1999, Karlee died in her sleep. We still don't know what really happened. We were in the middle of building a new house with handicapped accessibility. We decided to go ahead with our plans and created a completely accessible house. So what to do with it and our knowledge and experience with a child with a handicap?? I tried daycare for such children. Then one night I found a website which had information on all children with special needs who are available for adoption in the United States. I found a sweet little girl named Chelsey. She had cerebral palsy. Her bio said, Chelsey needs a family. Can you be her family? I said sure! Yes! Nine months later we were paper-ready. Chelsey had already been adopted. SUCH disappointment. But the adoption people knew

we were paper-ready and contacted us in January. A young lady was pregnant with a baby diagnosed with brittle bone disease. They asked if we were interested. I again turned to the internet for information. I found a support group for parents of children with brittle bone disease and asked these parents what they would do in my shoes. A lady in the group had brittle bone disease AND worked for an adoption group. She said to me, "If you decide not to take the brittle bone baby, I am representing a child in Europe, three years old, who has spina bifida." The next day she sent me Benal's picture. Two days later she sent me a video. Two WEEKS later we were visiting her! She was tiny, darling with big brown eyes and dehydrated. She was a charmer! We fell in love instantly. Benal's lesion on her back had not even been repaired and her hydrocephalus was left untreated. She basically is paralyzed from the hips down and actually does not have hip sockets. Her feet are deformed. When we met her she was nonverbal — wouldn't say a word. She also gagged on anything not pureed. We returned home to start the mountain of paperwork. Five months later we got to travel again to bring her home. Our facilitators were preparing to leave the orphanage, but we insisted that we get to see [another] child with spina bifida. Our attorney told us this is the room where they keep the most medically affected children (the to-die room — no kidding). And then we saw Nikki. She was left in a very small crib in a stifling hot room. No toys, no stimulation at all. She screamed when she saw us. They told us they only took her out of the crib once a day to feed and change her. I insisted that they take her out and let me hold her. Her resemblance to my Angel Karlee Rose was frightening. It took all my control to not start sobbing. She FELT like Karlee, heavy with low muscle tone. There was no way in the world we could leave her there. We insisted we talk with the orphanage director. Our attorney said we should take Benal home and think about this. We said NO WAY. So the director said she would consider us as a family for Nikki. Nikki's adoption took a YEAR.

> *(Katie, mom of Karlee Rose, Nikki, and Benal,*
> *who were born with spina bifida)*

The Gift of Your Child

Your child will change you.

When Gianna was first diagnosed, I truly believed that she was a great gift. No one has had as much impact on my life as she has. I pray every day that I will honor her life by trying to bring some good into this world. I used to be content to move in my own circles of close friends and family. Now, when God shows me a need, and I feel the impulse to respond, I don't hesitate to reach out. My heart yearns to do what I can to help mothers who are in a similar situation that I was in. These babies are truly a gift from God and each holds a unique purpose; by saving her baby, a woman learns to love unconditionally and this may be the very path to her salvation.

(Doreen, mom of Gianna who
was born with Trisomy 13 and holoprosencephaly)

Before Jonny's birth, I'd prepared announcements with a line from Elizabeth Barrett Browning: "God's gifts put man's best dreams to shame." I sent them proudly, adding a note about his extra chromosome and our great love for him. He's been a gift I never would have thought to ask for, bringing lessons I never knew I needed to learn. The greatest surprise is this: Our life together has been less about my helping him reach his potential than about him helping me reach mine.

(Barbara, mom of Jonathan, Jesse, Daniel, and Justin,
all of whom were born with Down syndrome)

You may find yourself helping others as a direct result of your child's birth.

We had told our [*European*] attorney that if ever they found a child with hydrocephalus, we would pay for the surgery for the shunt. They established a foundation called Shunt For Life because of this. While we were overseas adopting Nikki, the driver told us about an infant in Varna who needed a shunt. We gave him the cash, he drove back to Varna the next day, and little Vanya had successful surgery that week! She was one of a set of twins now available for adoption. My sister-in-law Cindy was taking care of a woman's mom during surgery. The woman's name is Kay. Kay told Cindy that they were applying to adopt a little boy who was missing one eye. Cindy connected Kay and myself and we became instant friends. They brought Josiah home from overseas. They got him an artificial eye and he's doing fine. Our adoption agency contacted them again and told them about a set of twin girls available for adoption in Varna. They accepted the twins. Kay mentioned that one girl had a shunt. I grabbed the phone and asked Kay, "Is her name Vanya????" "YES!!!!!!" Wow, what a true miracle! So months later they were able to bring the girls home. They are beautiful! And they renamed Vanya Mattea Rose. For my Karlee Rose whose spina bifida started us on a journey that continues to this day.

(Katie, mom of Karlee Rose, Nikki, and Benal,
all of whom where born with spina bifida)

Nathan was born with Menke's Disease. This photo of Nathan at age thirteen is the last photo taken of him before his death.

You will never know the extent of your child's influence on others:

- One doctor was amazed that a mother continued her pregnancy and gave birth to her daughter, knowing in advance that she would not survive more than a few days. Only in later years, when the doctor came to know the loving power of God, did he realize that knowing this mother and her baby were a significant part of his faith journey.

- One woman was working at a yard sale when a father, two children in tow, came to pay for his items. The older boy was carrying a small car and the younger one, in a stroller, was chewing on a rubber cartoon character. As the woman took the money, she noticed that the child in the stroller had the characteristic features associated with Down syndrome. When the little boy dropped his cartoon character and smiled up at the woman who picked it up for him, she had the distinct feeling that she was looking into the face of Jesus.

- When a girl with two artificial legs walked across the stage to receive her high school diploma, her class erupted into applause. She did not even know all the classmates who were cheering her, but they knew her.

In 1982 my daughter, Karen, was born with Down syndrome and a severe heart defect. Less than six months later she died of complications of pneumonia. Karen taught me things no teacher ever did: That life isn't fair — to anyone. That self-pity can be an incapacitating disease. That God is better at directing my life than I am. That there are more caring people in the world than I knew. That Down syndrome is an inadequate description of a person. That I am not "perfect" either, just human. That asking for help and support is not a sign of weakness. That every child is truly a gift from God. That joy and pain can be equally deep. That you can never lose when you love. That every crisis contains opportunity for growth. That sometimes the victory is in trying rather than succeeding. That every person has a special purpose in life. That I needed to worry less and celebrate more.

(Nancy, Karen's mom)

Your child was never given to you for you alone. Your child has a mission in life — to make the world a better place because he or she was in it. Your mission is to see that it happens.

Nick has a magnetic personality and strong character that has compelled countless people to express to me personally how much my son has inspired them. Nick's fifth-grade teacher even had a special award presented to Nick for being such an outstanding young man. How proud can a mother possibly be of a son who has not achieved walking on the moon but who is a positive influence on the lives of others who have not faced the hardships he has undergone?

*(Ashley, mom of Nick who
was born with spina bifida)*

Looking into Nathan's eyes was like looking into the eyes of an angel. It was like he could see into our souls. Quite a different experience than with our other children, even when they were babies. Nobody understands the blessings of children like this unless they have had the great gift of parenting or being close to them in some way. I will be grateful forever and forever.

*(Jennifer, mom of Nathan who
was born with Menke's Disease)*

As life unfolds, day to day, with all its sorrows and joys, trials and successes, frustrations and achievements, the mission is achieved. Go forward in faith, hope, and love. The journey has just begun, and the journey itself is a gift.

Appendix A — Books

Books for Additional Reading

Beck, Martha. *Expecting Adam: A True Story of Birth, Rebirth, and Everyday Magic.* New York: Berkley Books, 1999. When Harvard-educated Martha and John Beck learn that they are expecting a child with Down syndrome, the news plunges them into an alternate world where love means more than scholarship and joy comes not from doing, but from being. A rich, funny, starkly real warts-and-all story about the real world in which we all ought to slow down and smell the roses. *Expecting Adam* shows what an unimagined gift a child with a disibility can be, and how much the parents grow as a result of having such a child.

Burke, Peter. *Brothers and Sisters of Disabled Children.* London and New York: Jesssica Kingsley Publishers, 2004. This somewhat clinical book examines various responses of siblings to a brother or sister with a disability. Various case studies help parents understand the many different reactions children can have. The book contains several helpful suggestions.

Canfield, Jack, Mark Victor Hansen, Heather McNamara, and Karen Simmons. *Chicken Soup for the Soul — Children with Special Needs: Stories of Love and Understanding for Those Who Care for Children with Disabilities.* Deerfield Beach, FL: Health Communications, Inc., 2007. Many different vignettes from many different families.

De Vinck, Christopher. *The Power of the Powerless: A Brother's Legacy of Love.* New York: Crossroad Publishing Company, 1988. The story of Oliver de Vinck, whose thirty years of life with severe disabilities changed his brother and his family forever. The author also includes the stories of three other people with disabilities and details the many gifts they brought to their families and friends. *The Power of the Powerless* provides a rich perspective in looking back on a life challenged by disability.

DeYmaz, Linda. *Mommy, Please Don't Cry: There Are No Tears in Heaven.* Sisters, Oregon: Multnomah Publishers, 2003. A childlike picture book for Christian moms who have lost a child before, during, or after birth. Comfort and encouragement come through the message that the child is happy in heaven and awaiting mom. Biblical references to heaven are in the back of the book, which also contains two pages for recording personal thoughts.

Fuller, Nina. *Special Strength for Special Parents: 31 Days of Spiritual Therapy for Parents of Children with Special Needs.* Evansville, Indiana: GMAPublishing, 2006. As well as being both an inspirational speaker and author, Nina is also the mother of two daughters with Down syndrome. Using Scripture as a basis for her reflections, Nina takes the reader on a thirty-one day retreat that explores every facet of parenting a child with a disability. A real boost for parents who need a shot of encouragement and hope.

Gallagher, Peggy, Thomas H. Powell, and Cheryl Rhodes. *Brothers & Sisters: A Special Part of Exceptional Families*, 3rd Edition. Baltimore,

Maryland: Paul H. Brookes Publishing Company, 2006. An excellent book which details the many facets of siblings relating to their brother or sister who has a disability. Techniques, questions, practical advice.

Kingsbury, Karen. *Summer: Baxter Family Drama, Sunrise Series #2.* Carol Stream, Illinois: Tyndale House Publishers, 2007. One of a series of popular Christian novels, Summer tells the story of Ashley and Landon's third child Sarah, who is diagnosed in utero with anencephaly. The drama of the Baxter family unfolds around this news. While the story is fictional, the attitudes of the various family members are true to life, and Sarah's life is clebrated with realism and joy.

Klein, Stanley D., Ph.D., and Schive, Kim, Editors. *You Will Dream New Dreams: Inspiring Personal Stories by Parents of Children with Disabilities.* New York: Kensington Books, 2001. Sixty-three excellent vignettes and much good advice, each from a different parent. A truly personal account of many parents' individual responses to the human, funny, bittersweet experience of raising children with disabilities. Excellent resource section featuring agencies in nearly every state in the USA.

Lafser, Christine O'Keefe. *An Empty Cradle, A Full Heart: Reflections for mothers and fathers after miscarriage, stillbirth, or infant death.* Chicago: Loyola Press, 1998. This tender, small book combines Scripture verses on the right pages with short reflections on the left. While the Scripture is Christian, generally the reflections are universal. Parents who have lost a child will appreciate the insight and honesty of these brief, healing thoughts.

McCall, Ashli Foshee. *Beyond Morning Sickness: Battling Hyperemesis Gravidaruum.* Charlestown, South Carolina: BookSurge LLC, 2006. Hyperemesis Gravidaruum is a disease that causes excessive nausea in pregnant women. This book offers much practical advice, and shares several stories of women who had this condition.

Nugent, Madeline Pecora. *Having your baby when others say no! Overcoming the fears about having your baby.* Garden City Park, New York: Avery, 1991. Out of print but copies are currently available from CFP Holy Angels Gift Shop, 520 Oliphant Lane, Middletown RI, USA 02842-4600. Text also online at http://penitents.org/giftshophavingbaby.html. This self-help book is a guide to coping with the many problems that mothers and their unborn children may face, including disclosure of unplanned pregnancy, finding financial and other assistance, and making plans for the baby. A great help for parents who need practical guidance in difficult pregnancy situations.

Papazian, Sandy. *Growing Up with Joey: A mother's story of her son's disability and her family's triumph.* Santa Barbara, California: Fithian Press, 1997. *Growing Up with Joey* details one family's journey with their son who was born in 1977 with cerebral palsy and epilepsy. Although the first four years of Joey's life are more detailed than the remaining years, the author takes the reader up to Joey's seventeenth birthday. Even though medical treatments are constantly improving and every family's experiences are unique, the emotional ups and downs of a family with three other children will resonate with parents who face rearing a child with disabilities.

Reist, Melinda Tankard. *Defiant Birth: Women Who Resist Medical Eugenics*. North Melbourne, Victoria: Spinifex Press, 2006. The nineteen women whose stories and photos make up the bulk of this book were told never to get pregnant and/or to terminate their pregnancies. Some of the women were older or had physical disabilities; others were pregnant with children whose prenatal tests revealed disabilities. The book provides ample proof of society's move toward neonatal eugenics.

Snow, Kathie. *Disability Is Natural: Revolutionary Common Sense for Raising Successful Children with Disabilities*. Woodland Park, Colorado: BraveHeart Press, 2005. Kathie Snow, the mom of a child with cerebral palsy, begins with the statistic that 20 percent of the population have disabilities so disability is natural, as USA federal law states. Snow develops her ideas using a commonsense approach in sharing how parents can successfully and sometimes radically deal with differently abled children and with a society that wants to focus on their disabilities rather than their skills. For parents who want to raise independent, well-balanced children, this book is a must read.

Winter, Judy. *Breakthrough Parenting for Children with Special Needs*. San Francisco, California: Jossey-Bass, 2006. An excellent book for parents of children with disabilities. The book covers first reactions to a child who has differences and then escorts the parents through medical, educational, and familiar decisions from birth to adulthood. A practical, positive guide to parenting.

Wunnenberg, Kathe. *Grieving the Child I Never Knew: A Devotional Companion for Comfort in the Loss of Your Unborn or Newly Born Child*. Grand Rapids, Michigan: Zondervan Publishing House, 2001. A tender and delicate journal for parents who grieve prenatal or early infant loss. The book is written from a Christian point of view but has much good in it for those of other or of no religious background. Each short chapter contains an incident in the life of a grieving parent, a reflection, questions that assist in healing, and a place to record your personal journey. *Grieving the Child I Never Knew* validates a parent's grief.

Yorgason, Blaine M. *One Tattered Angel: A Touching True Story of the Power of Love*. Salt Lake City, Utah: Shadow Mountain, 2003. As told by her adoptive father, this heartwarming and amazing story of Charity Afton Yorgason gives deep insights into parenting a child with severe physical and mental disabilities. Born without a brain cortex, Charity weathered many health crises and alternated between bouts of pain and joyful, giggling days. The love of her family for her, and her for her family, carried them all through days of darkness and sunshine and brought gifts which would have come no other way.

Videos

Bittersweet: Stories of Open Adoption. Always Moving Pictures, 3349 Cahuenga Blvd. Suite 5, Hollywood, CA 90068, 310-393-7123 (office), 310-890-2520 (cell), email Steve@alwaysmovingpictures.com An excellent, fifty-three minute documentary featuring birth mothers, adoptive families, and children involved in open adoption. A top-notch, insightful film for parents considering an adoption plan for their child.

The Gift of Hope: The Tony Melendez Story. Vision Video, P.O. Box 540, Worcester, Pennsylvania, 19490, (800) 523-0226. Born in 1962 without arms, Tony is known worldwide for playing the guitar with his feet. This is his story.

My Little One (Mein Kleines Kind) An eighty-eight minute documentary of a baby born with Trisomy 18, made by his mother, who is a midwife. A touching story of a pregnancy from diagnosis in utero through birth. In German with English subtitles. The website (http://www.meinkleines-kind.de/) is in German but can be read in other languages.

Mooney, Matt. *99 Balloons.* A six-minute, online video of Eliot Mooney, who was born with an underdeveloped lung, a hole in his heart, and Trisomy 18. The video details the ninety-nine days of his life. A beautiful celebration of a child. http://www.ignitermedia.com/products/iv/singles/570/99-Balloons.

Snow, Benjamin. *Thumbs Down to Pity.* (Woodland Park, Colorado: BraveHeart Press, 2006). Benjamin Snow, who has cerebral palsy, made this sixty-second online movie. Benjamin is a capable young adult whose goal is to have people with disabilities be respected, not pitied. http://www disabilityisnatural.com/index-ben.htm.

Appendix B — Agencies

These links are a sampling of the great deal of information available via the internet and are intended as a starting point for research. While the following links are either supportive or noncommittal regarding carrying your baby to term, some of them may link to termination sites. Chapter Three of this book gives information on successfully using the internet to research information. (Note: These URLs were accurate when this book was published. If one is not working, search for the organization by name. The URL may have changed.)

Abortion (Termination of Pregnancy,
Pregnancy Induction to End Pregnancy)

Abortion Coercion — http://www.unfairchoice.info/

Abortion Information — http://www.clinicquotes.com/

Abortion Quotes — http://www.epm.org/articles/abortionquotes html/

Adoption

Adoption Blessings Newsletter — http://adoptionblessingsnewsletter.com/

Christian Homes and Special Kids — http://www.chask.org/

Jewel Among Jewels Adoption Network — http://www.adoptionjewels.org/

Special Needs Adoption — http://specialneeds.adoption.com/

Tree of Life — http://www.toladopt.org/

Anencephaly

Anencephaly Blessings from Above — http://healthgroups.yahoo. com/group/anencephalyblessingsfromabove/

Anencephaly Information — http://www.anencephalieinfo.org/

Breastfeeding

La Leche League — www.llli.org/

Carrying to Term

A Child of Promise — http://www.achildofpromise.org/

Be Not Afraid — http://www.benotafraid.net/. Stories and photos from parents who carried to term despite a serious prenatal diagnosis.

Carrying to Term pages — http://www.geocities.com/tabris02/

Carrying to Term after Negative Prenatal Diagnosis — http://carrytoterm.org/

Carrying to Term Support Pages — http://health.groups.yahoo. com/group/MiracleAngels/. Sharing board for those carrying to term.

My Child, My Gift: www.mychildmygift.com. Includes interactive forum.

Prenatal Diagnosis: Information and Stories — http://www.angelfire. com/ca/numberslady/

Prenatal Partners for Life — http://www.prenatalpartnersforlife.org/

Clothing

God's Tiny Angels — http://danettesangels.tripod.com/. Handcrafted clothing for premature babies.

Deafblindness

A–Z to Deafblindness — http://deafblind.com/. Many resources for those
who are both deaf and blind.

Disability

Alliance for Technology Access — http://ataccess.org/

Disability Is Natural — http://disabilityisnatural.com/

Mobility International USA — http://miusa.org/

National Dissemination Center for Children with Disabilities — http://nich-
cy.org/. Information on USA federal laws for children with disabilities.
Catalog of free resources.

Open Directory on Children with Special Needs — http://dmoz.
org/Home/Family/Parenting/Special_Needs_Children/

Doctors (these groups can help you locate doctors who
will support your decision to continue your pregnancy)

American Association of Pro Life Obstetricians and Gynecologists — http://
aaplog.org/

Catholic Medical Association — http://cathmed.org/

Christian Medical Association — http://cmdahome.org/

Pro-Life Maternal-Fetal Medicine — http://prolifemfm.org/

Down Syndrome

Down Syndrome Resource Center — http://www.aim.high.org/data/

Einstein Syndrome — http://einstein-sydrome.com/. Parent support for
Down syndrome.

National Down Syndrome Society — http://ndss.com/

Dwarfism

Little People of America — http://www.lpaonline.com/

Feeding

Feeding by G-tube — http://gtube.org/

Education

IDEA — Individuals with Disabilities Education Act — http://ed.gov/policy/
speced/guid/idea/idea2004.html

Learning Disabilities Association of America — http://www.ldaamerica.org/aboutld/parents/index.asp

Grief

Baby Steps — http://www.babysteps.com/

Claire's Friends — http://clairesfriends.org/

Elizabeth Ministry — http://elizabethministry.com/

Empty Cradles — http://empty-cradles.com/

Morning Light Ministry — http://morninglightministry.com/

My Forever Child — http://myforeverchild.com/. Keepsake items.

Share Pregnancy and Infant Loss — http://nationalshareoffice.com/

Hannah's Prayer Ministries — http://hannah.org/

Shrine of the Holy Innocents — http://www.innocents.com/. Click on the Shrine link in the left link column to memorialize your baby.

Heart Defects

Congenital Heart Information Network — http://tchin.org/

Hypoplastic Left Heart Syndrome (HLHS) Information — http://www.hlhsinfo.homestead.com/

Little Hearts — http://littlehearts.org/. Support for families of children with congenital heart defects.

Hydrocephalus.
See Spina Bifida and Hydrocephalus Category below

Limb Differences

First Step: A Guide for Adapting to Limb Loss — http://amputee-coalition.org/first_step/firststepv2_s1a12.html

Helping Hands Foundation — http://helpinghandsgroup.org/. Support groups for limb differences.

Youth in Motion — http://amputee-coalition.org/inmotion_youth.html/.
Magazine for youth with limb differences published by the Amputee Coalition of America.

War Amps Champ Program — http://waramps.ca/champ/home.html

Link Sites

Disability Resources on the Net — http://deafblind.com/disabili.html

Our-Kids — For Parents of Kids with Disabilities.— http://our-kids.org/. Website of helpful books on various conditions and links to many online sites on various disabilities.

Medical Information

Medical Dictionary — http://emedicine.com/asp/dictionary.asp.

National Library of Medicine Database — http://www.ncbi.nlm.nih.gov/sites/ entrez. Has many medical journal articles that can help parents find the latest treatments for specific conditions, as well as the physicians who perform them.

Milk Banks

To Donate Breast Milk — http://breastfeeding.com/all_about/all_about_ milk_banks.html

Moral Teaching

Charter for Health Care Workers, Pontifical Council for Pastoral Assistance to Health Care Workers, Vatican City, 1995 — http://wf-f.org/healthcare-charter.html

Parenting

Chromosomal Deletion Outreach — http://chromodisorder.org/CDO/. Matching parents of children with chromosomal deletion.

Exceptional Parent Magazine — http://eparent.com/

MUMS — http://www.netnet.net/mums/. Putting parents in touch with one another.

National Respite Locator Service — http://respitelocator.org/

Parent Advocacy Coalition for Educational Rights (PACER) — http://pacer.org/

Parents Helping Parents — http://php.com/

Technical Assistance Alliance for Parents Centers — http://taalliance.org/

Perinatal Hospice

Alexandra's House — http://alexandrashouse.com/. Perinatal hospice for dying infants and their families.

Hospice Care Network — http://hospicecarenetwork.org/

Perinatal Hospice Information — http://aaplog.org/perinatalhospice.htm

Photographs

Baby Angel Pics — http://babyangelpics.com/. This company can touch up photos of babies whose bodies have been disfigured by early death in utero or by the delivery process.

Prayer

Prayers for Life — http://penitents.org/prolifeprayer.html. Prayers for families experiencing problem pregnancies.

Problem Pregnancy Help

Pregnancy Care Centers — http://covenantnews.com/pregnant/

Pregnancy Help Center Referral — http://optionline.org/

Potter's Syndrome

Potter's Syndrome online support group — http://potterssyndrome.org/

Rare Diseases

National Organization for Rare Diseases (N.O.R.D.) — http://www.rarediseases. org/. Information plus rare diseases database. Includes organization list.

School

National Challenged Homeschoolers Association Network (NATTHAN) — http://nathhan.com/. Christian families homeschooling children with disabilities.

Individuals with Disabilities Education Act — http://ed.gov/offices/OSERS/ Policy/IDEA/index.html

Love and Learning — http://loveandlearning.com/home.shtml. Education at home for children with differences.

Special Reads for Special Needs — http://specialreads.com/. Reading and money management instruction for children who need extra help with these skills.

Wright's Law — http://wrightslaw.com/. Special education resources and advocacy.

Siblings

The M.I.S.S. Foundation — http://misschildren.org/. Helpful resources for siblings dealing with death.

Sibling Support Project — http://siblingsupport.org/. Materials for siblings of children with differences.

Spina Bifida and Hydrocephalus

Hydrocephalus Foundation, Inc. — http://hydrocephalus.org/

Spina Bifida Association — http://www.sbaa.org/site/c.gpILKXOEJqG/ b.2016945/k.2321/Spina_Bifida_Association_Web_site.htm

Spina Bifida Family Support — http://spinabifidasupport.com/

Spina Bifida and Hydrocephalus Association of Ontario (SBH [Spirit, Breakthrough, and Hope]) — http://sbhao.on.ca/

Trisomy

Rainbows Down Under — http://members.optushome.com.au/karens/. Information and support on many Trisomy conditions.

Support Groups for Chromosomal Deletions — http://kumc.edu/gec/support/chromoso.html. Groups for every chromosomal deletion known.

S.O.F.T. — http://trisomy.org/index.php. Support and information on Trisomy 13, Trisomy 18, and related disorders.

Appendix C—Scriptural and Inspirational Quotations

Biblical Passages

God is our refuge and strength, a very present help in trouble. Ps 46:1
❧

Cast your burden on the Lord, and he will sustain you; he will never permit the righteous to be moved. Ps 55:22
❧

For it was you who formed my inward parts;
  you knit me together in my mother's womb.
I praise you, for I am fearfully and wonderfully made.
  Wonderful are your works;
that I know very well.
  My frame was not hidden from you,
when I was being made in secret,
  intricately woven in the depths of the earth.
Your eyes beheld my unformed substance.
In your book were written
  all the days that were formed for me,
  when none of them as yet existed. Ps 139:13–16
❧

[T]he Lord does not see as mortals see; they look on the outward appearance, but the Lord looks on the heart. 1 Sm 16:7
❧

Take care that you do not despise one of these little ones; for, I tell you, in heaven their angels continually see the face of my Father in heaven. Mt 18:10
❧

[T]oday that I have set before you life and death, blessings and curses. Choose life so that you and your descendants may live, loving the LORD your God, obeying him, and holding fast to him; for that means life to you and length of days. Dt 30: 19–20
❧

[B]ecause we look not at what can be seen but at what cannot be seen; for what can be seen is temporary, but what cannot be seen is eternal. For we know that if the earthly tent we live in is destroyed, we have a building from God, a house not made with hands, eternal in the heavens. 2 Cor 4:18–5.1
❧

So it is with the resurrection of the dead. What is sown is perishable, what is raised is imperishable. It is sown in dishonor, it is raised in glory. It is sown in weakness, it is raised in power. 1 Cor 15:42–43
❧

For this perishable body must put on imperishability, and this
mortal body must put on immortality. When this perishable body
puts on imperishability, and this mortal body puts on immortality,
then the saying that is written will be fulfilled:
'Death has been swallowed up in victory.'
'Where, O death, is your victory?
  Where, O death, is your sting?'
The sting of death is sin, and the power of sin is the law. But
thanks be to God, who gives us the victory through our Lord Jesus
Christ. 1 Cor 15:53–57
      ও

In all your ways acknowledge him, and he will make straight your
paths. Prv 3:6
      ও

[Love] bears all things, believes all things, hopes all things,
endures all things. Love never ends. 1 Cor 13:7–8
      ও

We know that all things work together for good for those who
love God, who are called according to his purpose. Rom 8:28
      ও

I consider that the sufferings of this present time are not worth
comparing with the glory about to be revealed to us. Rom 8:18
      ও

You have turned my mourning into dancing;
  you have taken off my sackcloth
  and clothed me with joy,
so that my soul may praise you and not be silent.
  O Lord my God, I will give thanks to you for ever. Ps 30:11–12
      ও

[H]e will wipe every tear from their eyes. ·
Death will be no more;
mourning and crying and pain will be no more,
for the first things have passed away. Rv 21:4
      ও

Be strong, and let your heart take courage,
  all you who wait for the Lord. Ps 31:24
      ও

But Zion said, "The Lord has forsaken me,
  my Lord has forgotten me."
Can a woman forget her nursing-child,
  or show no compassion for the child of her womb?
Even these may forget,
  yet I will not forget you.
See, I have inscribed you on the palms of my hands;
  your walls are continually before me. Is 49:14–16
      ও

Other Inspirational Passages

Those we love are with the Lord, and the Lord has promised to be with us. If they are with Him, and He is with us, they cannot be far away. — *Peter Marshall*
ॐ

You are valuable because you exist. Not because of what you do or what you have done, but simply because you are. — *Max Lucado*
ॐ

Some Loves last a Moment,
Some Loves last a Lifetime,
Sometimes a Moment is a Lifetime.
— *author unknown*
ॐ

There is nothing to be afraid of if you believe and know that the cause for which you stand is right. You are ready to face anything and you face it with a humble smile ... because you know that all of eternity stands with you and the angels stand beside you.
— *Martin Luther King, Jr.*
ॐ

What we have once enjoyed and deeply loved we can never lose, for all that we love deeply becomes part of us. — *Helen Keller*
ॐ

God promises a lamp unto our feet, not a crystal ball into the future. — *Max Lucado*
ॐ

Don't measure the size of the mountain; talk to the One who can move it. — *Max Lucado*

(All selections from "Comfort for parents of an anencephalic baby" http://www.anencephalie-info.org/e/comfort.htm. Bible translations from New Revised Standard Version, Anglicized Edition)

Appendix D

If You Have Had a Termination

You may have already terminated a pregnancy. This book may have recalled certain memories and caused you pain. It is important to accept what has happened and move on from there.

- Certain words were likely used to soften or mask the facts. You were asked or told that you had to decide when deciding was not necessary.
- The words "pregnancy termination" or "pregnancy induction" may have been used. However, natural hormones will induce all pregnancies eventually and every pregnancy will terminate on its own.
- Most pregnancies terminate with a living baby. The intention of your "pregnancy termination" or "induction" was to produce a dead baby. The commonly applied term for this is abortion.
- You were probably given much encouragement to end the pregnancy and very little to continue it.
- You may have felt unable to cope with carrying your baby to term and making plans for your child.
- You may have wanted the situation to be over quickly.
- You may have felt that your decision would prevent your child or others from suffering.

Whether or not you thought your choice was good, right, and/or loving then, you now are thinking differently.

Now you can see your role in the decision to terminate. Despite what could have been great pressure, probably no one actually forced a termination upon you as it is forced upon women in China. Nevertheless, even if you made the decision somewhat freely, you had many accomplices. They must be acknowledged, too.

> Those who encouraged the woman to have an abortion, to kill that baby, by words, action, or sins of omission, or who did the gruesome work of the abortion, have an equal share in that guilt. One consequence of this for the people involved is disunity. Those who collaborate in abortion and who do the grisly work, or who promote it in any way, have a deep aversion for one another that comes out in all kinds of disordered behavior.
>
> *(Joan, mom of an aborted child)*

> After delivering my dead baby, we were given that opportunity to hold her. My husband couldn't bring himself to hold her or even look at her. I held her little body in my arms and I cried. I still didn't realize how wrong this all was. The clinic staff and the doctor complicated matters by making everything seem normal. What happened to us, and what

continues to happen to others every day, is the furthest from normal as you can possibly get. They take pictures of the baby and give you an urn for the ashes. The doctor talks about the grieving process, and uses terms like "miscarriage abortion" to somehow make you believe your child was meant to die. Everything is twisted. The financial cost for "making your dreams come true," as is advertised on one website, whose abortionist does late abortions, is substantial. For us it was over $7,000.00, which we charged on an American Express card. Blood money — we gave him $7,000.00 and he killed our baby.

(Francesca, mom of Josephine, diagnosed with multiple disabilities and who died by saline injection to the heart prior to "pregnancy induction" at thirty-six weeks gestation)

You will have discovered that those who encouraged you to "induce your pregnancy" or supported the "termination" do not want to hear any more about it. You are on your own in dealing with the memories and regrets.

We abort for convenience only to find out that we will never have convenience again. The doctors and everyone else involved in abortion all bank on one aspect — that you will forget. That you will forget what you have done to your poor innocent child.

(Eric, father of Emmanuelle, diagnosed with a brain anomaly, who died by saline injection to the heart prior to "pregnancy induction" at twenty-four weeks gestation)

Yes, you probably agreed to terminate the pregnancy. At the same time, recognize that you probably acted in confusion and under duress. Even if you seemed certain at the time and at peace, you were responding to a shutdown of your maternal instincts. Whatever your exterior demeanor was, inside you were desperate. Desperate people often make poor choices that they later regret.

While we were in Kansas we were told over and over that we were doing the right thing. Ultimately, it was our decision to make, but never once were we told of the joy our child could bring, even through her pain. Never once did anyone mention any other options. I realized later that we were given our "options" with the basic understanding that we shouldn't have the baby. Oh, how I wish I had the courage to stop everything and go home. Unfortunately, I was too weak and dazed to help my child. I will never "get over" this; I go on and I do have a happy life. But I will never be able to change the fact that I am responsible for the death of my child. It's something that I can only learn how to live with.

(Francesca, mom of Josephine, diagnosed with multiple disabilities and who died by saline injection to the heart prior to "pregnancy induction" at thirty-six weeks gestation)

Acknowledge your decision. Ask forgiveness of your child and name him or her if you have not yet done so.

If you are a person of faith, seek out a member of the clergy and share your story.

You may also want to assist other women in continuing their pregnancies. You can do this via online web support groups and by volunteering at pro-life crisis pregnancy centers. You can find a center near you via the internet at optionline.org or by calling 800-395-HELP. If you are not in the United States, you can locate a pro-life crisis pregnancy center near you at covenantnews.com/pregnant/ or by phoning the Catholic diocese in your area and asking for referral. While most pro-life pregnancy centers are not run by the Catholic Church, the Catholic diocese usually has a list of the pro-life pregnancy centers on hand.

You may wish to assist with or establish a perinatal hospice for women whose babies are diagnosed with fatal or very severe conditions in utero. The perinatal hospice's intent is to support the parents and allow the baby to be born and to die naturally. Since some people oppose this, speak to a Catholic or Christian hospital, which may be more supportive of this idea.

You cannot bring your child back. Nor can you undo the past or erase a decision. But you can move forward. One woman who had an abortion is now helping other women and men who, like her, regret their abortion choices. "My abortion was evil," this woman says. "God did not will it. But God can bring good out of evil."

Work and, if you have faith, pray to bring some good out of your child's death so that he or she will not have died in vain.

APPENDIX E — GRIEF JOURNEY

The Journey by Mindy Wilsford

In this expression of grief I used a journey through a mountain range to describe the ups and downs, the length, and the incredible frustrations of my grief journey. Many people have told me that it accurately describes their grief as well.

Before we go through a loss like this, we assume that grief is like falling into a deep hole. We think we will start climbing a ladder and as we get closer to the top things start getting brighter and brighter and we keep feeling better and better until we finally step out into the sunshine where the birds are singing and beautiful music is playing and our grief is over and we are then officially "over it."

Instead, I have found it is like being plunked down into the middle of a mountain range. We start on the top, with the breathtaking view, when life is wonderful. We are just walking along, basking in the sun and the beautiful scenery when suddenly we fall off a cliff. Now we are lying in a deep, deep valley: bruised, confused, hurt, scared, and lonely. We soon realize that there is no easy way out, no rescue in sight. The only way out is to do it ourselves.

So we start working our way up the mountainside, sometimes walking, sometimes crawling, and often stumbling. It is very hard, very discouraging, and very exhausting work. Finally we reach the top and see the sun again for a while. Maybe the top will be flat and we'll get to spend a little time up there enjoying it, or maybe it is very steep and as soon as we get there we have to start back down the other side into the next valley again.

The one thing we notice is that there are mountains as far as the eye can see. Somehow, we have to make our way through them if we are ever to get out. That thought can be overwhelming and cause us to give up for a while. But eventually we realize once again that the only way out is to keep going, so we start again: down one mountain and up the next. And sometimes on the journey, after a particularly hard stretch, we think, "I'm so glad I finally made it through that." And then we stop and look around and realize that we've been here before! All this work and we've gone in a circle and we're going to have to do it all again!

And sometimes as we are climbing, we look up to see if we are getting any closer to the top, and we see a boulder heading our way. If we are fortunate, we manage to avoid it. But usually we can't, and it hits us head-on and sends us tumbling back down to the bottom.

Sometimes when we are in the deepest part of the valley, we just sit, exhausted. And we might notice some things around us that we never saw before: flowers and animals and a gentle breeze in the cool of the valley. There is a world down in the valley that we never even knew existed, and there is beauty in it.

And sometimes at night, when all is quiet, we can hear the others who are in the valley weeping. And it is then that we realize that we are not alone, that others are making this journey too. And we realize that we share an understanding of the journey and of the world of the valley that most others don't. And it gives us strength to start the climb all over again.

Sometimes as we are climbing the mountain, a helicopter may come by with some of our friends in it. Seeing us struggling up the mountain, they shout encouraging things like, "I know just what you're going through; I went on a hike once." And "At least you have your other kids to make this climb so much easier." And "You are so strong; I know I couldn't make this climb." Or they ask, "When will you finally get over these mountains and be yourself again?"

And we try to tell them about the journey and the world of the valley, but the sound of the helicopter drowns us out and they can't hear us. They throw down some food to give us energy, and it does, but some of it just pelts us on the head and makes the climb even harder. And then they leave, and we breathe a sigh of relief that we can get back to our climb in peace.

As we make this journey, we start to notice that we are becoming a little bit stronger. When we get to the rough patches we now see that we are shaken but don't always fall. We find that sometimes we can walk upright now, instead of just crawling. And sometimes we can see a rough spot ahead and manage to find a better way around it. And once in a while we crest a mountain and see that the top is very flat and very beautiful, and we get to spend quite a while resting and recovering on the top before starting down again. And we notice that we are getting closer to the edge of the mountains; they seem to be getting a little smaller. The mountains are not as tall, and the valleys are not as low or as wide. In fact, we can now see the foothills, and it gives us hope.

And throughout this journey, we see the others who are traveling it as well, sometimes at a distance, and sometimes up close. And we encourage each other to keep going and to watch out for certain things. We talk about the journey and the world of the valley. *Finally, someone else who understands!* And we cry together when it is just too hard. And sometimes, we catch a glimpse of someone who has made it to the foothills. And we are so excited for them, and we become even more determined to keep going because someday, we too will make it to the foothills.

So my point is this: everyone starts on a different mountain. No two journeys are the same. Some people spend a lot of time in the valley at first, and some have more time on top of the mountain. But we will all be both on the mountains and in the valleys. And we will all someday make it to the foothills. I promise.

The Circus by Mindy Wilsford

I wrote this story to describe how difficult it is for those who have lost a baby to see other healthy babies being born.

The class had just gotten the news: they were going to the circus! Most had never been to the circus, but a few had, and they told the others what it was like and how much fun it would be. Each day they learned something new about the circus: studying the animals they would see, reading about the entertainment, and discussing the food. They learned the history of the circus and watched a video that one of their classmates had taken when he was there last year.

Soon it was all everyone was talking about. Day by day the excitement grew as the date approached. Then, a week before the big day, one of the students was informed he wouldn't be able to attend. No reason; he had done nothing wrong; he just couldn't go. And even though he pleaded and cried, the teacher would not relent.

The student was stunned and crushed. "How could this be? Surely there must be a mistake. I'm supposed to go, too."

But it was not to be. He would not be going to the circus.

The other students in the class felt bad for him and commiserated for a while. But soon they tired of it and went back to excitedly discussing the upcoming circus. "After all," they thought, "it's sad that he can't go, but there's nothing we can do about it. Besides, he can always go next time."

Unsure of how to act, he tried to keep a brave face and pretend that he was OK. He listened to them talk about the circus and even joined in sometimes, sharing about what he had learned. But sometimes he couldn't do it anymore, and he had to leave to hide the tears that were welling up in his eyes. And when the day of the circus arrived, he was totally lost. "Should I pretend I don't care? Should I go and wish them well? Should I just stay home and cry?"

His mother told him he needed to be a big boy and be happy for everyone else who was getting to go. So he joined the class, reluctantly, wishing he were anywhere else but there. And he did his best not to ruin anyone else's fun.

It was very obvious that he was not enjoying anything about the day, but everyone else, preoccupied with the excitement of the event, didn't notice it. Most were simply so exuberant that they just chattered on and on about it. When they got to the gate, as everyone jostled for position to get in, he quietly stepped aside. And after they went in, their laughter echoed in his head as he fought that sad, sick feeling. It just wasn't fair!

All he could do was watch them, listen to them, and hear from them. HE should be at the circus, too. That was the loneliest day of his life.

When the day was over, he stood there, forcing a smile, feigning interest, as they told about the day's events and showed him pictures. They were so excited and eager to tell about their day, and all he could think about was how hard it was to not be a part of it. He deserved to go as much as they did; how it hurt to not be able to! But somehow they didn't seem to understand that, as they continued to talk about the circus and show their souvenirs. He felt like such an outsider; he wanted so badly to share in their joy, but he just couldn't. It was still too hard. Someday he would be able to, but not yet. And he looked forward to that time because no one would be happier about it than him.

I'm so sorry we didn't get to go to the circus.

Appendix F: Sibling Stories

These stories are intended to be shared with your other children, to initiate discussion about brothers and sisters with disabilities.

Melody Fruit

(To help adolescents and teens understand the reasons for carrying this child to term)

On all the small planet of Jesera, Lissanda was the only kingdom that could grow Melody Fruit. Kings and queens, princes and princesses, dukes and duchesses placed orders months in advance for Melody Fruit. The farmers of Lissandra grew prosperous and efficient in producing enough Melody Fruit to satisfy the entire Jesera market.

Young Orans had learned the art of growing Melody Fruit from his father who had learned it from his father who had learned it from his father as far back as generations could remember. He knew well the signs of healthy fruit on the sprawling vines. First the green buttons which budded into five-petal, sky-blue blossoms. Fertilized by the honeybees of Lissandra, these flowers produced small orange bumps which swelled like balloons to become glimmering orange orbs the size of basketballs. After one hundred days, one by one, ripe Melody Fruit would ease away from the vines. Then farmers like Orans would pack them ever so carefully and fill their orders. Kings and queens, princes and princesses, dukes and duchesses would carefully lift the Melody Fruit from their soft packing material and would toss them skyward where they would be caught by the winds and gently open into five-pointed orange stars. As they opened, the most exquisite melodies would burst from the opening fruits — melodies of dance and song, of sun and laughter, of scented pine and cinnamon, and of glittering, glistening rivers.

Occasionally a strange twist of fate struck a Melody blossom and the fruit budded into a wizened black bump. If left to grow, no glimmering orange orb would ever develop but only a wrinkled, misshapen ball. Back as far as anyone could remember, farmers plucked these aberrations from the vines and threw them aside. As they did so, the stricken Melody Fruit would open, emitting a dirge of death and darkness, fear and despair, end without hope.

Orans had never seen a stricken Melody Fruit fall from the vine of its own accord. He wondered if it would happen. So one year when one of his vines developed a stricken fruit, he did not pluck it early but allowed it to grow. Every day he watched it, becoming more accustomed to its darkness and its wrinkles as the days drifted on. As his workers tended the vines, they would remark to him, "Sir, there is a stricken fruit on that vine. Shall we pluck it off?"

"No," Orans would say.

"But it is stricken. It is taking nourishment from the other Melody Fruit."

"I do not see them being harmed," Orans noted.

"They must be harmed. Surely some of the vine's strength is going into a fruit that will be forever tainted."

"I want to let it grow until it leaves the vine itself," Orans would explain.
"But why?"

"Because that is the way it was with Melody Fruit before man began to cultivate them."

The workers would shrug and move on to their tasks, certain that their employer was, perhaps, a bit crazy.

Every day Orans came to check his vines. Every day the Melody Fruit grew, the orange ones into larger and larger balloon-like, glittering fruit and the wizened one into larger and larger shriveled fruit. Yet Orans sensed that the stricken fruit was even more different than it appeared. When Orans touched the shriveled fruit, his soul shivered with emotions he had never felt before. They puzzled him.

After one hundred days, the fruits gently pulled away from their vines. The fully ripe orange orbs were plucked, packed, and shipped until only one wizened, dark ball was left in Orans's field. As the sun was dipping low in the sky and the workers were departing, Orans picked the wrinkled mass from the earth and studied it. Surely it was a Melody Fruit. Here and there he could see glimmers of light and slathers of orange. He held it long, feeling the inexplicable magic of its difference. Then, as if from the Melody Fruit itself, Orans heard a silent command. "Release me."

"Be released," he called as he tossed the shriveled ball skyward where the winds could catch it. Gently the dark skin opened into five sagging points and a song poured out. The melody was one that Orans had never heard before, not from any of his other Melody Fruits or those of his father or grandfather. It was a song of pain conquered by joy, of despair drowned in victory, of death reborn into life. The song surrounded Orans and pierced to his soul like a golden arrow, searing there virtues he had long desired but never attained — patience, courage, trust, love.

Gradually the Melody Fruit dissipated into the air as all Melody Fruits do. The song faded as all melodies fade. When all was silent and the sky clear, nothing remained of the Melody Fruit. Yet in Orans's soul for forever were patience, courage, trust, and love.

Orans would never be the same.

Questions:

1. What traits did people associate with Melody Fruit?
2. Why were Melody Fruit so valuable?
3. What occasionally happened to a Melody Fruit? What did farmers do to these blighted fruits?
4. What did Orans decide to do with a blighted Melody Fruit?
5. What reactions did he get when he made his decision?
6. Why did Orans decide to let the Melody Fruit grow?
7. What do you think Orans meant when he said, "Because that is the way it was with Melody Fruit before man began to cultivate them"? Do you think Orans was saying that, in nature, some Melody Fruit were blighted and that there must have been a reason for that, even if farmers did not know what it was?

8. What was the gift of the blighted Melody Fruit?
9. What gifts do you think your brother or sister might bring to our family? Do you think they might surprise us?
10. Do you think the gifts Orans received from the blighted Melody Fruit might be some of the ones we will receive as a family, from this brother or sister? Why do you think this?

Hannah Bear's Baby Brother

(To get a young child to confide any negative feelings about a sibling who has changed the family)

Hannah Bear had a good life with Mother and Father Bear. They taught Hannah to climb trees and to find honey. Every day, Mother, Father, and Hannah took a stroll through the forest down to the stream. There Hannah would lie in the water and watch the fish swim by. Sometimes she would catch one.

One day Mother Bear did not come out of her cave. Father Bear explained that Mother was not feeling well. That evening, Hannah heard a weak whimper from the cave and Mother called out, "Baby Bear is here." Hannah and Daddy rushed in to see Baby Bear. He was small and black and wet. And he whimpered. Mother explained that soon he would be climbing trees and finding honey and lolling in the stream with Hannah.

Many weeks went by, but Baby Bear did not grow much. His legs did not seem to work well. He never walked out of the cave and so he could not climb a tree or find honey or loll in the stream. Mother Bear stayed home with Baby all the time. Now Hannah and Father Bear had to walk the woods alone.

Hannah tried to play with Baby Bear, but he only looked up at her and whimpered. She would nudge him with her nose and he would laugh. But he could not play.

Hannah loved Baby Bear, but sometimes she wished he could play with her like other baby bears. Sometimes she wished he would die so that Mother Bear could go down to the stream again. Sometimes she wanted life to be like it had been. But she did not want to worry Mother and Father. She never told them how she felt about Baby Bear.

One day Father Bear said, "Hannah, a penny for your thoughts."

Hannah stopped chasing a butterfly long enough to tell Father that she had no thoughts.

"Hmm," Father said, "that is very odd because I have lots of thoughts. Sometimes I think how much fun Mother and you and I had before Baby Bear was born. Sometimes I am sorry those days are gone."

Hannah came up to Father Bear and nuzzled his big, black paw. "Sometimes I feel like that, too," she said.

"I know," said Father, "and I am glad you told me. Do you know what I think? I think we can work to make those days happen again."

"How?" asked Hannah. "Baby Bear cannot walk with us and he cannot be left alone."

"Then we will carry him," Father said. "I am big and strong and Baby Bear can ride on my back."

"But he will fall off," Hannah said.

"Mother Bear can tie him on my back with vines."

"Do you think Mother will let us try?"

"We can ask her," Father said. And so they did.

Mother agreed. And now Father and Mother, Hannah and Baby stroll through the forest. They climb trees and eat honey. They loll in the stream and watch the fish go by. Baby Bear still cannot walk. But he can blow bubbles. And he and Hannah laugh and laugh and laugh.

Questions:

1. What was life like for Hannah before Baby Bear came?
2. How did life change for Hannah?
3. What were Hannah's feelings about Baby Bear? Did these surprise you?
4. Why did she not want to talk about them?
5. How did Father sometimes feel about Baby Bear? Did his feelings surprise you?
6. What feelings do you have about _____ (name of sibling)? Are they like Hannah's?
7. Do you think Mommy and Daddy sometimes feel like Father Bear?
8. What do you wish we could do with _____ (name of sibling)?
9. How do you think we could try to make that happen?

Appendix G: Catholic Teaching on Early Induction of Labor

National Catholic Bioethics Center on Early Induction of Labor

BOSTON, MA— The National Catholic Bioethics Center wishes to assist individuals and institutions working with the ethical issue of early induction of labor. The following is the NCBC position regarding the application of Catholic moral teaching and tradition to the issue.

The application of Catholic moral teaching and tradition to this issue is directed toward two specific ends: (1) complete avoidance of direct abortion, and (2) preservation of the lives of both mother and child to the extent possible under the circumstances. Based upon these ends, the Ethical and Religious Directives for Catholic Health Care Services provides directives which set the parameters for the treatment of mother and unborn child in cases of high-risk pregnancies:

47. Operations, treatments, and medications that have as their direct purpose the cure of a proportionately serious pathological condition of a pregnant woman are permitted when they cannot be safely postponed until the unborn child is viable, even if they will result in the death of the unborn child.

49. For a proportionate reason, labor may be induced after the fetus is viable.

The principle of the double effect is at work in each of these two directives. Actions that might result in the death of a child are morally permitted only if all of the following conditions are met: (1) treatment is directly therapeutic in response to a serious pathology of the mother or child; (2) the good effect of curing the disease is intended and the bad effect foreseen but unintended; (3) the death of the child is not the means by which the good effect is achieved; and (4) the good of curing the disease is proportionate to the risk of the bad effect. Fulfillment of all four conditions precludes any act that directly hastens the death of a child.

Early induction of labor for chorioamnionitis, preeclampsia, and H.E.L.L.P. syndrome, for example, can be morally licit under the conditions just described because it directly cures a pathology by evacuating the infected membranes in the case of chorioamnionitis, or the diseased placenta in the other cases, and cannot be safely postponed. However, early induction of an anencephalic child when there is no serious pathology of the mother which is being directly treated is not morally licit, emotional distress notwithstanding. Early induction of labor before term (37 weeks) to relieve emotional distress hastens the death of the child as a means of achieving this presumed good effect and unjustifiably deprives the child of the good of gestation. Moreover, this distress is amenable to psychological support such as is offered in perinatal hospice. Lastly, induction of labor before term performed simply for the reason that the child has a lethal anomaly is direct abortion.

[Author's Note: The induction of labor before term performed simply for the reason that the child has a nonlethal but adverse health condition is also direct abortion.]

The mission of the National Catholic Bioethics Center, founded in 1972, is to defend the dignity of the human person through research, education, publishing, and consultation in the health and life sciences.

For further information, contact:

The National Catholic Bioethics Center
6399 Drexel Rd
Philadelphia, PA 19151
(215) 877-2660 (phone)
(215) 877-2688 (fax)
Website : www.ncbcenter.org

Glossary

ABS

An abbreviation for amniotic band syndrome (see definition).

achondroplasia

Dwarfism compatible with life.

ADD

Abbreviation for attention deficit disorder (see definition).

attention deficit disorder

a condition in which an individual experiences differences in behavior, attention, and comprehension.

adoption, closed

An adoption agreement in which birth parents and adoptive parents agree to have no contact with each other.

adoption, open

An adoption agreement in which birth parents and adoptive parents agree to have contact with each other.

adoption, private

An adoption agreement made among a lawyer, birth parents, and adoptive parents without involving an adoption agency.

AFP

Abbreviation for alpha-fetoprotein test (see definition).

alpha-fetoprotein

A substance made in the liver of an unborn baby. Certain concentrations in the mother's blood indicate that the child may have a disability.

alpha fetoprotein test

A test to check the level of alpha-fetoprotein (AFP) in a woman's blood.

alveolar ridge

The bony ridge of the gumline containing the teeth.

amnio

Short name for amniocentesis (see definition).

amniocentesis

Prenatal test in which a needle draws a sample of the amniotic fluid from which the unborn baby's cells are then tested for genetic or other differences.

amnio-infusion

Fluid installation into the amniotic cavity through a catheter, done to provide more fluid around the unborn baby.

amniotic band syndrome

A condition in which fibrous amniotic bands entangle the unborn baby's limbs or digits, causing amputation or malformation.

amniotic bands

Fibrous strands of membrane that stretch into the amniotic cavity.

amniotic cavity

The cavity in the womb in which the unborn baby develops.

amniotic fluid

Watery liquid surrounding and cushioning an unborn baby in the womb.

anencephaly

Most common neural tube defect in which the unborn baby's brain does not develop in whole or in part.

apnea

Suspension of external breathing.

aprosencephaly

Malformation of the nervous system and skull associated with low survival rate.

ASD
Abbreviation for autism spectrum disorders (see definition).

atrium (left, right)
One of the upper chambers of the heart. The left atrium receives oxygenated blood; the right atrium receives deoxygenated blood.

auricle (left, right)
An older name for the left and right atrium of the heart (see atrium).

autism
A developmental disorder that prevents individuals from acting in what is considered to be a normal manner.

autism spectrum disorders
Impairment in thinking, feeling, language, and the ability to relate to others, ranging from mild to severe.

bag valve mask
A handheld device used to assist or initiate breathing in a patient.

bagging
Helping a patient to breathe by using a bag valve mask.

beta strep
Abbreviation for group B streptococcus (see definition).

bilateral renal agenesis
Also known as Potter's Syndrome (see Potter's Syndrome).

bladder exstrophy
A birth defect in which the bladder is exposed, inside out, and protrudes through the abdominal wall.

body jacket
A support that fits over the chest, abdomen, and upper pelvis, used to support an unstable or recently fused spine.

brain stem
The part of the brain connected to the spinal cord.

brittle bone disease
A group of genetic bone disorders that causes weak bones that break very easily.

calvarium
The cranium without the face.

CAT scan
Abbreviation for computed (axial) tomography (CAT or CT scan). Generates a three dimensional image of the internal organs.

cebocephaly
A facial anomaly characterized by a small, flattened nose with a single nostril situated below incomplete or underdeveloped closely set eyes.

cerebellum
The portion of the brain in the back of the head between the cerebrum and the brain stem.

cerebral hemispheres
The two specialized halves of the brain, each of which is responsible for different abilities.

cerebral palsy
A general term for a group of permanent brain injuries.

cerebrum
The largest portion of the brain.

cheilognathopalatoschisis
Physical condition involving a cleft lip, alveolar ridge, and palate.

chorioamnionitis
Serious infection of the placental tissues.

chorion
Outermost membrane around an unborn baby.

chorionic villus sampling
Prenatal test in which a needle or catheter is used to obtain a sample of the villi found on the outermost membrane of the baby.

choronic villi
Short, hairlike outgrowth of a membrane that fosters transfer of nutrients from the mother's blood to the baby's blood.

chromosomal deletion
Loss of a segment of DNA from a chromosome (and hence from the entire organism).

chromosome
Component in a cell that contains genetic information.

cleft lip
An abnormal fissure of the lip which failed to close during development in the womb.

cleft palate
A congenital fissure at the roof of the mouth forming a passageway between the mouth and nasal cavities.

cloacal exstrophy
A severe birth defect in which much of the abdominal organs are exposed, the anus may be closed, and the genital organs may be split.

clubfoot
A birth defect of the foot in which the foot turns inward and downward.

club leg
Congenital defect of the foot and lower leg.

CMTC Syndrome
A syndrome involving skin mottling and which may also include asymmetry of the body, developmental delays, seizures, and other difficulties.

comfort care
Providing love, pain relief, and comfort to a dying baby but without medication, surgery, or equipment to prolong life.

congenital amputation
Loss of a body part that occurs in utero.

cortex
The external layer of gray matter of the cerebrum and cerebellum.

CPAP
Continuous positive airway pressure, used to treat sleep apnea.

cranium
Part of the skull that encloses the brain.

cribriform plate
Part of the bone that separates the nasal cavity from the brain.

crista galli
Thin sheet of bone that rises into the brain.

CT scan
See CAT scan.

CVS
An abbreviation for chorionic villus sampling (see definition).

cyclopia
A congenital defect involving the development of only one eye and a missing or misshapen, misplaced nose.

cystic fibrosis
A recessive genetic disorder affecting the mucus lining of the lungs, leading to breathing problems and other difficulties.

developmental disability
A condition that causes a person to develop at a slower rate than the norm.

dilation and curettage
Opening (dilation) of the cervix and removing the contents of the uterus including the baby if one is present.

D&C
Abbreviation for dilation and curettage (see definition).

DNA
The material inside the nucleus of cells that carries genetic information. The scientific name for DNA is deoxyribonucleic acid.

Down syndrome
Syndrome that causes slowed growth, distinctive facial features, and some degree of mental retardation. Also called Trisomy 21.

dura
The outermost, toughest, and most fibrous of the three membranes (meninges) covering the brain and the spinal cord.

dwarfism
Short stature. Adult height four feet ten inches or less.

dysplasia
Any abnormal development of tissues or organs.

early induction
Euphemism for abortion. The act of bringing on labor contractions very early in pregnancy.

early intervention
Early mental and physical stimulation to help a child develop his or her full potential.

eclampsia
A complication of pregnancy resulting from high blood pressure.

edema
Excessive accumulation of fluid.

Edwards syndrome
Another name for Trisomy 18 (see definition).

encephalocele
Protrusion of the brain through an opening in the cranium.

epidural
Common method of administering anesthesia during labor. A small amount of anesthesia is inserted into the dura space near the spinal cord.

epilepsy
A disorder of the brain that results in recurrent, unprovoked seizures.

ethmocephaly
An uncommon facial anomaly consisting of a proboscis separating narrow-set eyes, one or both of which may be abnormally small, and with an absent nose.

feeding pump
A small machine that automatically controls the amount of formula being delivered through a feeding tube.

feeding tube
A tube used for long-term feeding or to supplement the nutritional intake of a patient.

folic acid
One of the B vitamins especially important for a woman to take before conception to help prevent neural tube defects in her unborn baby.

fundo/g-tube
A tube that brings nutrients into the upper portion of the stomach.

GBS
Abbreviation for group B streptococcus (see definition).

gene
The fundamental physical and functional unit of heredity.

genetic screening
The process of analyzing DNA samples to detect the presence of a gene or genes associated with an inherited disorder.

genetic testing
Analyzing an individual's genetic material to determine predisposition to a particular health condition or to confirm a diagnosis of genetic disease.

gray matter
Another name for the cerebral cortex, or the "thinking matter" of the brain.

group B streptococcus
A common type of bacteria found in the vagina or rectum of up to 40 percent of pregnant women; may cause serious problems in the baby.

H.E.L.L.P. syndrome
A pregnancy complication which requires management of blood clotting and may indicate a need to deliver the baby early.

hemorrhage
Bleeding or flow of blood either internally or externally.

holoprosencephaly
Congenital brain disorder also involving facial differences.

HRHS
See hypoplastic right heart syndrome.

hydrocephalus
An accumulation of fluid within the skull.

hydronephrosis
Abnormal enlargement of a kidney.

hypochondroplasia
Mild dwarfism; features become apparent at two to three years.

hypoplasia
The underdevelopment of a tissue or organ.

hypoplastic left heart syndrome
A congenital anomaly in which the left ventricle is either very small or missing; the most common lethal condition in congenital heart disease.

hypoplastic right heart syndrome
Hypoplastic right heart syndrome is a congenital heart defect in which the right ventricle of the heart fails to grow and develop appropriately.

IEP
Abbreviation for "Individual Education Plan," an educational plan created to fit the needs of a specific child.

induction of labor
The use of artificial means to start the process of childbirth.

intubation
Inserting a tube into the trachea of a patient who is not breathing so as to foster breathing.

in-utero operation
Operation on the unborn baby through the wall of the uterus, to correct a defect prior to birth.

limb differences
Any abnormalities of the arms or legs.

magnetic resonance imaging
Nonsurgical method used for rendering an image of the inside of an object.

maternal serum screening test
Another name for triple screening test (see definition).

meningomyelocele
Congenital defect of the central nervous system of the baby. Membranes and the spinal cord protrude through an opening or defect in the vertebral column.

Menke's Disease
A congenital defect manifested by short, sparse, poorly pigmented kinky hair and associated with failure to thrive, physical and mental retardation, and progressive deterioration of the brain.

microcephalus
A condition causing a small head with a sloping forehead that prevents normal development of the brain, resulting in a mental disability.

milk bank
A place where human breast milk is kept for distribution to babies in need of it.

miscarriage
A spontaneous abortion; a pregnancy that terminates on its own prior to birth.

miscarriage abortion
A euphemism intended to make an induced early abortion sound like a spontaneous, natural miscarriage.

MRI
Abbreviation for magnetic resonance imaging (see definition).

multiple marker test
Another name for triple screening test (see definition).

muscular dystrophy
A genetic disorder of the muscles that causes them to become weak.

neural tube defect
Birth defects of the brain and spinal cord.

neurofibromatosis
A genetic condition that affects the nervous system, muscles, bones, and skin.

neurosurgeon
A doctor who specializes in surgery on the brain, spine, and other parts of the nervous system.

NICU
Acronym for Newborn Intensive Care Unit, the hospital unit where the sickest babies are kept for constant monitoring.

nuchal fold
Translucent area in the skin on the back of the baby's neck. A thick nuchal fold is associated with Down syndrome.

OI
Abbreviation for osteogenesis imperfecta (see definition of brittle bone disease).

oligohydramnios
The medical term for a condition which involves having too little amniotic fluid.

omphalocele
Presence of congenital outpouching of the umbilicus containing internal organs in the unborn or newborn infant.

open adoption
See "adoption, open."

osteogenesis imperfecta
Technical name for brittle bone disease (see definition).

oximeter
A device worn on the finger or earlobe that can measure levels of oxygen in the blood painlessly.

oxygen tent
A canopy placed over the head and shoulders or over the entire body of a patient to provide oxygen at a higher level than normal.

palliative care
Care that offers comfort, pain relief, and love to a dying person but does not employ life-sustaining medication, surgery, or equipment.

Patau syndrome
Another name for Trisomy 13 (see definition).

PDD
An abbreviation for pervasive spectrum disorder (see definition).

perinatal hospice
A program of comprehensive palliative care for babies diagnosed in utero with fatal conditions and involving their parents and families.

perinatologist
Physician who specializes in the care of high-risk pregnancies.

pervasive developmental disorders
Another name for autism spectrum disorders (see definition).

pervasive spectrum disorder
Diagnosis along the autism spectrum. See also autism.

pH
From potential of Hydrogen. The measure of the acidity or alkalinity of a solution.

pH probe
Twenty-four-hour pH monitoring to identify certain diseases or abnormal conditions in the body.

polyhydramnios
A term for too much amniotic fluid.

posterior urethral valves
An abnormality of the urethra where the urethral valves (small leaflets of tissue) have a narrow, slit-like opening that partially impedes urine outflow. Reverse flow occurs and can affect all of the urinary tract organs.

Potter's Syndrome
A fatal combination of birth defects characterized by the absence of one or both kidneys and underdeveloped lungs.

preeclampsia
Serious pregnancy condition involving high blood pressure in the mother, water retention, and high protein levels in her urine.

pregnancy interruption
A euphemism for induced abortion. Interrupting a pregnancy so as to cause the death of the baby.

pregnancy reduction
A euphemism for selective abortion of one or more children in a multiple pregnancy.

pregnancy termination
A euphemism for abortion. Ending the pregnancy so as to cause death of the baby.

premaxilla
The paired bones forming the front of the upper jaw.

prosencephalon
One of the three primary vesicles of the embryonic brain.

prosthesis
Artificial extension that replaces a missing body part.

protocol
A precise and detailed plan for the management of a specific situation or condition.

respirator
A device that supplies oxygen to assist in artificial breathing (respiration).

respiratory distress
Difficulty in breathing.

respite care
Services that provide people with temporary relief from tasks associated with caregiving.

saline injection (abortion)
Injection of saline solution into the amniotic fluid or the heart of an unborn baby, to cause death, prior to induction of labor.

scoliosis
Lateral curvature of the spine.

selective reduction
Killing one or more of multiple unborn babies so as to leave fewer babies alive in the womb.

sepsis
Infection.

shunt
An artificially created passageway that allows excess fluid to flow harmlessly out of an area.

sickle cell anemia
A recessive genetic disorder in which red blood cells take on an unusual shape, leading to other problems with the blood.

sickle cell disease
Another name for sickle cell anemia (see definition).

skeletal dysplasia
Differences in the bones causing shortened limbs and stature. Dwarfism.

spina bifida
A birth defect resulting from the incorrect development of the spinal cord.

stillborn
A baby that dies naturally in utero or during the labor and delivery process.

syndactyly
A condition in which webs of skin grow between the fingers and/or toes.

termination of pregnancy
A euphemism for abortion. Ending a pregnancy by bringing on early labor so that the baby will be born dead.

thanatrophic dwarfism
Deadly form of dwarfism due to extreme rib shortening that compresses the lungs.

thanatrophic dysplasia
Another name for thanatrophic dwarfism.

toxemia
Also called preeclampsia (see definition).

toxoplasmosis
An infection caused by a parasite that can lead serious illness or death in the unborn child.

triple screening test
A blood test that is performed usually between the fourteenth and eighteenth weeks of pregnancy to determine the probability of the baby having Down syndrome.

trisomonial
Having to do with Trisomy.

Trisomy
Possessing three copies of a particular chromosome instead of the normal two copies.

Trisomy 13
The presence of three #13 chromosomes, also known as Patau syndrome, involving multiple abnormalities, many incompatible with life.

Trisomy 18
The presence of three #18 chromosomes, also known as Edwards syndrome, involving multiple malformations and mental retardation.

Trisomy 21
More commonly called Down syndrome. Caused by an extra copy of all or part of chromosome 21. See also Down syndrome.

tube feed
The baby's food is given through a tube in the nose directly into the stomach.

urethral obstruction malformation sequence
Syndrome that causes abnormalities in the abdominal organs and wall.

ventricle (left, right)
One of the two lower chambers of the heart.

ventricular septal defect
A hole between the two ventricles of the heart.

ventriculomegaly
Increased size of the ventricles in the brain.

water on the brain
Common term for hydrocephalus (see definition).

white matter
Nerve tissue that is paler in color than gray matter. Contains nerve fibers with large amounts of insulating material (myelin). Does not contain nerve cells.